MOTHER
TERESA

MOTHER TERESA
Love Stays

CHRISTIAN FELDMAN

Translated by Peter Heinegg

A *Crossroad Book*
The Crossroad Publishing Company
New York

The Crossroad Publishing Company

Originally published as *Die Liebe bleibt: Das Leben der Mutter Teresa,* copyright © 1997 by Verlag Herder, Freiburg im Breisgau

Printed in the United States of America

Picture Credits: *cover:* Catholic News Service; *inside photos:* KNA-Bild, Frankfurt am Main, except for pp. 14 and 18, Robert Serrou, *Mutter Teresa: Eine Bildbiographie* (Freiburg im Breisgau, 1980), and p. 85 © Peter Wesely, editorial staff "thema Kirche," Vienna.

Library of Congress Cataloging-in-Publication Data

Feldman, Christian.
    [Mutter Teresa. English]
    Mother Teresa : love stays / by Christian Feldman ; translated by Peter Heinegg.
    p. cm.
    ISBN 0-8245-2221-6 (paperback)
    1. Teresa, Mother, 1910–1997. 2. Missionaries of Charity – History. 3. Nuns – India – Calcutta – Biography. 4. Calcutta (India) – Biography. I. Title.
BX4406.5.Z8F4513 1998
271'.97–dc21
[B]   97-45766
                                                      CIP

This printing May 2016

Contents

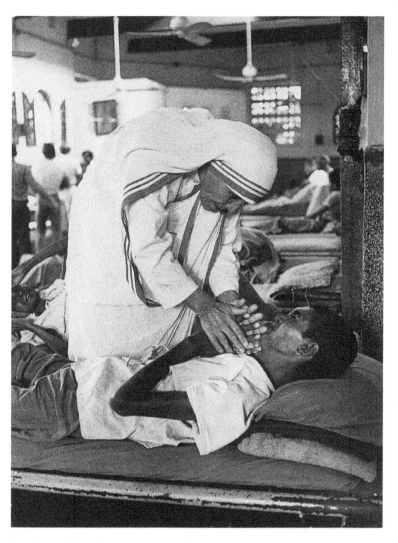

In the Hall for the Dying in Calcutta.

Foreword

Mother Teresa has entered into the life that knows no end. She knew that we live in a world where light and darkness are found right next to each other. Her life was an invitation to decide for the light.

I met her in the most varied situations, among others when I lived with some of my brothers among the poorest of the poor in India.

During one of her visits to Taizé we were anxious to compose a joint appeal, which is as valid now as ever: "In Calcutta one can find visible homes for the dying, but in Western societies many young people live in invisible homes for the dying. They are marked by broken-off human relations or anxiety over the future. This is the root of skepticism and discouragement: Why live at all? Does life still have a meaning?"

Among the hours I spent with her the most precious were in Rome back in 1984, when we were asked to work together to design the inaugural celebration of the World Youth Congress.

For Mother Teresa prayer was the source of a love that sets the heart on fire. She was aware that community in God leads us out of ourselves and into a transfiguration of our person. So the question arises: how can we ease the mental and physical sufferings of men and women on this earth?

FRÈRE ROGER SCHUTZ

Taizé
September 10, 1997

Prologue

In the sewer system of Calcutta, with its 320 miles of pipes, reservoirs, and pumping stations, the smell of rotting flesh is sometimes so awful that the sewer workers go on strike. This happens, they say, because of the bloated corpses that family members throw into the sewers when they can't afford the wood to cremate their dead with.

Calcutta is the city as nightmare. A stinking grave, a hell bursting at the seams, where masses of doomed, emaciated people fight for a few square yards of breathing room. In this metropolis of fifteen million people the authorities have officially registered several thousand different slums.

They are crammed in between modern high-rises and shopping centers. They pop up unexpectedly like ghost villages between rows of terraced houses. Picturesque palaces lie cheek by jowl with garbage dumps swarming with figures of wretchedness.

Above the endless slums floats a stifling stench of putrefaction. The jute sacks or plastic tarps offer little protection from the torrential monsoon rains.

And yet the Calcuttans who call such derisory shelter home may well consider themselves lucky: the *really* poor people live on the sidewalks and traffic islands. They are born there, live there, sleep there, and die there.

On wet mud paths, in filthy shopping arcades these human wrecks camp out, exhausted, starving, marked with cholera or malaria. Flies cluster in their open wounds.

A whimper is heard from an overflowing garbage can. A young woman in a white sari cocks her ear for a moment, then hurries

to the garbage pile and pulls out a naked baby, a handful of skin
and bones, which she protectively gathers into her arms.

A few yards farther on, the white-robed helpers find a ghostly
skeleton, its parchment-like skin stretched over sharply protrud-
ing bones, the remnant of a human being that still seems to have
some life left in it. The maggots have already begun to strip away
his skin. The girls in saris carry the old man off to a shadowy
hall, feed him, and wash his poor, feces-smeared body. An old
woman removes the worms from his wounds.

"How can you bear my stink?" the dying man barely manages
to whisper, in stunned amazement.

"That's nothing at all compared with the pain you must be
feeling," his attendant answers.

"You're not from around here," the old man marvels. "The
people here don't do what you do."

Even as he dies he attempts to smile. "Bless you."

"No," the woman in the sari replies, with a smile, "bless *you*,
because you suffer with Christ."

The nondescript woman at the deathbed, giving the wretched
bundle of humanity his dignity back at least in his last moments,
was Mother Teresa, the founder of the Missionaries of Charity.

In India (and elsewhere), there may be a lot of talk about plans
for development. "But," as she always said, "not much happens.
We need people who roll up their sleeves and aren't too delicate to get their fingers dirty in the gutter, to tear rags away
from festering sores, to clean the feces, urine, and vermin from
dying people, to feed lepers and pick up the corpses of babies
from garbage pails. Anyone who can do that will always find a
welcome with me."

MOTHER TERESA

1

"I'm an Officer Too"

The Call to Follow Christ into the Slums

The remarkable thing is that she was normal.
— A fellow nun from Dublin

She must have been a lively child, absolutely *not* a boring, cerebral little angel. Her brother, Lazar, recalls her as incredibly bright and verbal, "always sure of herself, sharp, never at a loss for words, and afraid of nobody."

Back then the future Mother Teresa was still known as Agnes Gonxha Bojaxhiu. She was born into a solidly middle-class Albanian family on August 26, 1910, in Skopje. The city was still under Turkish rule at the time; later it became part of Yugoslavia, and it's now the capital of newly independent Macedonia. In old Skopje the cross and crescent stood face to face. Muslim minarets soared alongside the Church of the Holy Redeemer. The town had been part of the Ottoman empire for five hundred years.

As Albanians and Catholics, the Bojaxhiu family belonged to a double minority. Mother Teresa's later staunch clinging to her convictions and her dogged perseverance have their roots here. Her father had a very successful career. He ran an architectural firm and became a co-owner of a flourishing construction company. When he died, Agnes was only nine years old. Their mother had to raise her son, Lazar, and her two girls all by herself. She had a practical turn, and opened a fabric and embroidery store.

Mother Teresa as a young woman.

Early photos show Agnes as a distinctly pretty girl with some-what dreamy eyes. Like very few other Albanian girls in Skopje, she went to the high school, where she showed a talent for music. She had a strikingly pure soprano voice, sang in the parish choir and in a Catholic choral group. She shone at concerts as a soloist and in duets with her sister. On outings with her girl friends, she usually took along an accordion or a mandolin.

Agnes wasn't thinking of a life in the convent just yet, al-though she was deeply interested in the work of the missionaries. Albanian Catholicism was rather deeply rooted in tradition; so naturally the Bojaxhiu household felt a lot of enthusiasm for spreading the kingdom of Christ all over the world — which was how Rome defined the missions in those days.

When Pope Pius XI introduced the feast of Christ the King in 1925 (to signal the rejection of secularized public life, but also in response to the totalitarian claims to power by the rising forces of fascism) Agnes was just fifteen. She eagerly devoured stories about the Yugoslavian Jesuits who were toiling in the Ganges delta of Bengal and in the Himalayas.

Three years later she herself decided to spend her life in the Bengal missions. Her big brother was dumbfounded. "How can you become a nun?" he wrote her in dismay. "Do you know what you're doing, sacrificing yourself forever, burying yourself alive?"

"I'll never forget her answer," he recalled years later. "I had just gotten out of the military academy in Albania and had re-cently been promoted to lieutenant. I was tremendously proud and extremely happy. "You make so much of yourself," she wrote him, "as an officer in the service of a king of two million people. Well, I'm an officer too, but in the service of the king of the world. Which one of us is right?"

We can already hear the voice of the classic Mother Teresa, as people would soon get to know her: at once self-conscious and humble, unwavering to the point of pigheadedness — and disarming in her apparent naiveté. She quickly convinced her brother. He admitted that her decision was basically quite logical in a family that had always helped the poor and outcast.

As Lazar says, "I remember how my mother once heard about a poor woman from Skopje, who was suffering from a tumor. She had nobody to look after her. Her family didn't want to have anything to do with her; they refused to help her in any way and threw her out, all because of some trivial business. My mother took her in, fed her, and cared for her till she was cured. So you see, 'Teresa' didn't just suddenly show up out of nowhere."

The High School for the Daughters of the Bourgeoisie

Agnes had an extraordinarily hard time breaking away from her parents' house, where she had been very happy. On November 29, 1928, she entered the Congregation of Loreto, better known as the "English Ladies," a teaching order whose members lived by the Jesuit rule.

Their foundress, Mary Ward, came from ancient Yorkshire nobility and was a stubborn, contrary person like her future Albanian disciple. Around the beginning of the seventeenth century she gathered together a few daring women friends and created a mobile task force to work with young people and provide pastoral care, working in "the world" without cloister or habits. She set up day schools for girls from the lower classes and developed a forward-looking pedagogy: dedication to the individual instead of a rigid schema, joy in learning instead of compulsion and whippings.

To be sure, their energetic, direct piety, oriented as it was to earthly needs, seemed just as suspicious as the new order's independent style of working. The papal nuncio Pallotta thought that such activities, with no male leadership, were extremely dangerous "for this sex so inclined to error." High-ranking English clerics wrote furious letters complaining to Rome; and one influential Jesuit patronizingly noted, "All well and good — but zeal puffs up; and after all they are only women."

The history of the founding of the congregation that Agnes Bojaxhiu entered in 1928 has its tragic features. The strict Roman ban on calling the rebellious Mary Ward the founder of the English Ladies wasn't lifted until 1909. But when Agnes arrived in the Rathfarnham Convent in Dublin, where she spent her first few months as a nun, she found a vital community. Within a few decades nuns from Rathfarnham had founded forty schools in the United States, Canada, and Australia.

Even today the motherhouse of the Loreto nuns in Dublin strikes the visitor as a Victorian castle, a gigantic edifice one could easily get lost in, awe-inspiring and not very cozy. Her fellow sisters found the young Albanian woman rather shy and introverted — which wasn't surprising since she scarcely spoke a word of English yet. "The remarkable thing is that she was normal," noted one of the Dublin nuns, which sounds like a compliment.

Agnes had no time at all to settle down. Within a few weeks she was sent to India, to the novitiate in Darjeeling, seven thousand feet up in the Himalayas. The British had founded the city as a summer resort; and at the time that Agnes was being initiated into the mysteries of religious life, the governor of Bengal and the rich upper class of Calcutta would regularly take refuge in Darjeeling to escape the burning, sticky heat. They went out horseback riding, dined in the club, drank tea on the immaculate green lawn of the government palace, nonchalantly enjoying life English-style on the roof of the world: from Darjeeling a caravan road leads across snow-covered mountain passes to Tibet.

In 1931 Agnes Bojaxhiu made her temporary vows as a nun — the permanent vows wouldn't come till 1937 — and took the name of Teresa. She liked and respected "little" St. Thérèse of Lisieux, with whom she shared a number of traits: stubbornness, a penchant for simple solutions, and a stormy passion for God.

Mother Teresa as a teacher in St. Mary's High School.

The newly minted Sister Teresa was sent to St. Mary's High School, run by her order in Calcutta, over four hundred miles away, where she spent the next twenty years teaching geography and history and rose to be principal of the school. The five hundred girl students came from the thin bourgeois upper crust of Calcutta. By Bengalese standards the convent–boarding school was a pleasant place to stay, with its carefully groomed lawns and well-trained girls in neat school uniforms.

Teresa, who meanwhile had learned to speak fluent Hindi and Bengali, was an outstanding instructor. Teaching was her favorite activity — as she later confessed in an interview, years after she had founded the Missionaries of Charity and no longer had high school girls, but young nuns sitting at her feet. She had managed to acquire leadership qualities not just as a school principal. She also directed the Daughters of St. Anne, an Indian congregation connected to the Loreto nuns.

The Slum behind the High School Walls

Back then India's dwindling little Catholic minority (1.7 percent of the population) bore the stamp of the potent financial support it got from Europe and the United States: a situation that hasn't changed much to this day. Christian educational institutions and hospitals enjoy high status, but the elite Catholic schools generally accept only the children of well-to-do parents.

Bishops' residences and seminaries often look like palaces — and this in a country where every other person lacks the basic necessities of life. Only in recent decades has the path been taken to a poor church, with young priests beginning to go into the slums and Christian families sharing the life of the downtrodden poorest of the poor. Meanwhile priests and bishops have emerged from the ranks of the *dalits*, the pariahs, who read the Gospel as a highly political message of liberation and who fight to overcome the inhuman caste system.

There was no way Sister Teresa could have remained blind to all this. Right behind the walls of the high school stretches an enormous slum with the perverse name of Moti Jheel, Pearl Lake, and its pestilential smell has always wafted onto the campus. Sister Teresa took a handful of her students, armed them with iodine and bandages, and marched through the slum. She met the poor, helped them as best she could, dragged food supplies and clothing into the cheerless huts, made herself useful in the modestly supplied local hospital — and had a guilty conscience when she went back home to her handsomely furnished convent.

God, as Teresa kept sensing more and more acutely, wanted more from her. Prayer, compassion, a few visits — that wasn't enough. Her outings to Moti Jheel struck her as ridiculous and pointless. For a while she had fetched two dozen girls from the slum, brought them into the high school and taught them. But the ragged creatures felt so ill at ease in the school's refined atmosphere that they soon slipped away. Obviously the Christ of the Loreto nuns was relevant only for the rich.

On September 10, 1946, the thirty-six-year-old Teresa was on an overnight train ride when once again she decided to "drop out," to add a still harder choice to the choice she had already made for a hard life in the order. "I had to leave the cloister and help the poor by living among them," was her sober way of describing the wave that burst over her. "I heard the call to give up everything and follow Christ into the slums, to serve him among the poorest of the poor. I knew it was his will, and I had to follow him."

Dear God, you great healer,
I kneel before you,
but every perfect gift
must come from you.

I beg you, give
skill to my hands,
keenness to my understanding,
and sympathy and gentleness to my heart.
Lend me the determination,
the strength to take upon myself
a part of the burden of my fellow men and women,
and true knowledge of the honor
that falls to my share.
Take away all falseness and
and all worldly longing
from my heart,
so I can trust you
with the simple faith of a child.

"Conversion" on the Night Train

Precisely dated "conversions," like the one on September 10, 1946, aren't so unusual in the history of Christianity.

In the dilapidated little church of Portiuncula Francis of Assisi heard the words with which Jesus sent out his disciples to preach: "Go and proclaim that the kingdom of heaven is at hand.... Take no bag for your journey, nor two tunics, nor sandals, nor a staff...." Francis was thunderstruck: "That's what I'm looking for!" he cried. He threw away his shoes, put on the brown cowl of the mountain shepherds and went off to wander through the villages, singing and preaching, an odd bird crazy with happiness.

With Augustine the whole thing was supposedly prompted by

a fit of depression in his garden and the monotonous singsong of a child next door: "Take and read, take and read...." Augustine got up, fetched a volume with the letters of Paul, opened it, and stumbled onto the passage in Romans: "Not in reveling and drunkenness, not in debauchery and licentiousness, not in quarreling and jealousy. But put on the Lord Jesus Christ...." He calmly went to a friend and told him about it. In the days that followed he broke free of all his ties, quit his teaching post, sold all the property he had inherited from his father, and built a commune for like-minded persons, a combination of monastery and philosophical academy.

On the night of November 23, 1654, Blaise Pascal, the brilliant mathematician and engineer, had an overwhelming experience: "From around 10:30 in the evening till half an hour after midnight, fever." He jotted this down on a slip of paper that he sewed into the lining of his jacket and always carried it around with him like a relic: "God of Abraham, God of Isaac, God of Jacob, not of the philosophers and scholars. Certainty, certainty. Joy, joy, joy, tears of joy.... May I never be separated from him!"

Of course, behind such snapshots lies a long rugged process of wrestling that can go on for years, with phases of despair and setbacks. Conversions often take one's whole life — but they seem to be concentrated in this sort of single experience that turns one's entire existence upside down. For Mother Teresa it came in a railway compartment between Calcutta and Darjeeling.

"It was a call within my vocation," was how she herself classified that night. "It was a second vocation."

Was she thinking about that night when much later on she attempted to describe the meeting between Mary and the angel of the Annunciation? "The Prince of Peace longed to come down to earth, and made use of an angel to bring the good news: the Creator is becoming a child. He felt drawn by a young girl who was nothing in the eyes of the world.... She looked at the angel (she must have been very surprised, never having seen an angel before) and asked: How is that? What are you saying? I don't understand your words; they have no meaning for me. But the angel said simply that Christ — through the power of the Holy Spirit — would be formed in her."

"God took on a little body," Teresa continues, "such a little body. And we find it so hard to become little. But Jesus tells us: 'Unless you become like little children, you shall not enter into the kingdom of God.' Mary knew that, and answered: 'Yes, behold, I am the handmaiden of the Lord.'"

A Thirty-Seven-Year-Old Dropout

At first the archbishop of Calcutta turned down Teresa's request to leave the convent. No doubt he thought that a European woman wouldn't be accepted in the slums. India was, after all, in turmoil. The British were getting ready to grant the country its independence. Wild emotions were boiling over against everything European; a merciless civil war was on the point of breaking out between Hindus and the Muslim minority.

Archbishop Perier, a Jesuit, was a European himself, but a man who could see beyond the narrow confines of traditional missionary work. He felt that the church's only chance for survival once India was independent lay in a consistently Indian Catholicism. Twenty years before Vatican II (1944), in a talk that created quite a stir, he had argued against "every kind of narrowness and exclusiveness" in the missions. Future priests, he said, had to be familiar with Indian culture and philosophy. Precisely because he was open-minded, like Teresa, Perier had to take a skeptical view of her plans: perhaps they were just one more notion imported from Europe.

Besides, there already was such a bewildering variety of women's orders. Wouldn't it be enough to intensify the work of the Daughters of St. Anne among the poor? They spoke Bengali, wore native Indian dress, and lived in extreme simplicity. But to Teresa this tried and tested unit wasn't sufficiently mobile. And even these relatively hardened angels in human form never approached the living wrecks rotting away on garbage dumps and in the worst corners of the slums.

Teresa readily understood the archbishop's misgivings. "He couldn't have reacted any other way," she said. "A bishop can't just trust any nun who comes along to present her arbitrary proposals under the pretext that it's the will of God." Teresa never had problems with church authorities, even when they tried for one reason or other to put the brakes on her élan. Her fidelity to Catholic authority can most likely be explained by her modesty. "Am I, a little nun," she seemed to be asking, "wiser than Mother Church with her two thousand years of experience?"

There was no change, however, in the stubborn way she fought for her ideas, once she had gotten something into her head: humbly but unwaveringly Teresa repeated her request one year later when millions of refugees were pouring out of the newly created nation of Pakistan into Calcutta, and the city had practically burst wide open.

This time, equipped with permission from the archbishop and the superior general of the Loreto nuns, she went off to Rome — and got an immediate reply: Pope Pius XII approved her intention of living among the poor, "with God as the only leader and protector." Her students prepared a melancholy feast to bid her farewell. "We sang some beautiful things in Bengali," one of them recalls: "They were songs of goodbye. The children gave her a present, and everybody cried. I think she went from the party to the church, and from there she just left. We never saw her again."

Teresa exchanged the habit of the Sisters of Loreto for the sari worn by poor Indian women, white with a blue border, costing around a dollar. On August 18, 1948, she stood completely alone in front of the convent wall, with no money, no place to live, no

training as a nurse or social worker, and no detailed plans — but feeling sure that "God is going with me. This is his work."

Life is beauty, admire it.
Life is bliss, enjoy it.
Life is a dream, make it a reality.
Life is a challenge, face it.
Life is a duty, fulfill it.
Life is a game, play it.
Life is precious, be careful with it.
Life is wealth, guard it.
Life is love, rejoice in it.
Life is a puzzle, penetrate it.
Life is a promise, keep it.
Life is sadness, overcome it.
Life is a hymn, sing it.
Life is a struggle, accept it.
Life is a tragedy, struggle with it.
Life is an adventure, risk it.
Life is happiness, earn it.
Life is life, defend it.

"Don't Kill It, Give It to Me"

The Children of the Garbage Dump

It was hard. But she wanted it to be hard.
— Sister Bernard

In Patna Teresa took some basic courses with the American Medical Missionary Sisters and learned about hygiene, nursing the sick, and midwifery. The sisters ran a hospital that enjoyed the highest reputation in the university town on the Ganges. Like Teresa, the mother superior there had gone her own way, astonishing the Vatican with her request to open a surgical and gynecological station.

Back in Calcutta again, Teresa went off into the Tiljala slum — one of the most notorious places in the city — and moved in with a family of seven. She gathered together a few children from the neighborhood and taught them the alphabet by scratching out the letters in the mud with a stick. There were no chairs, benches, or tables.

She showed the children how to wash, and she gave each of them a piece of soap — an unknown luxury in Tiljala. At noon each day she distributed milk to her protégés. She went out and begged food for the half-starving families. She cared for the sick, visited the hospitals.

More than once the lonely sister was in danger of breaking down. What good was her helpless rushing from emergency to emergency when measured against the omnipresent concentrated misery that weighed down on Calcutta, crushing all hope?

In Hell There Is No Hope

The slums of the nightmare-city: under a ramp leading to a bridge inventive beggars build their absurd dwellings. With mud and dirt from the street they have molded paper-thin walls and covered them with torn sacks of tea. A few yards above their heads flows a roaring stream of traffic.

In the slums of Calcutta, it is claimed, every third person lives off garbage. People collect broken glass and plastic bags; they trade in dirty bits of scrap iron; they weave mats out of green coconut shells; they paste bags together out of old newspapers.

And yet there is beauty in this city. The flower market glows in an unearthly colorful splendor of dark red and gaudy yellow, rich purple and dazzling orange. The inner courtyards of the Bengal palaces have been compared to the palazzi of Genoa and Florence. Government buildings from the Victorian era, the Neo-Gothic St. Paul's Cathedral, and the many gorgeous gardens bring to mind the days when Calcutta was the second-largest city in the British Empire and a governor general had his residence here.

But at the gates of the feudal palaces, still inhabited by the rich, beggars loiter; and in the wretched streets millions of people wait for a predictable death in the dirt. In this life, as they well know, they will never get a chance. Teresa, the lonely nun, set forth to change a little bit of this cheerless reality; but she soon plunged into bitter despair. What was the sense of making a breach here and there in the walls of desolation and violence? Who got helped when a tiny little corner of this hell was made a friendlier place, so long as the same dreary grayness prevailed along so broad a front?

"I learned a difficult lesson," she later recalled, thinking back to this phase of profound depression. "Poverty must be so hard for the poor. When I was looking for a house for my settlement, I walked around and around until my arms and legs ached. I thought how much pain they have to endure in soul and body when they're out looking for a place to sleep, for something to eat, and security. That was how the security of Loreto came to appear to me a temptation.... Leaving Loreto was the greatest sacrifice for me, the hardest thing I've ever done. It was much harder than leaving my family and my country to enter the order. Loreto meant everything to me."

The Parents Were Horrified

Despite her unswerving stance Teresa might not have persevered — had it not been for the young girls who thought the way she did, who joined her and fought as hard as she against the desperate need that cried out to them from every street corner. Most of them were Teresa's former students from the high school.

A few months after she had begun work in the slums, the first recruit came knocking on her door: Subhasini Das, a graceful, pretty Bengali girl, nineteen years old, extremely shy, but with tremendous will power. She was so fond of Mother Teresa that when she took her vows she chose Teresa's baptismal name and was henceforth known as Sister Agnes.

One year later she already had twenty-six companions. These young women had joined her in looking after the poverty-stricken people of Calcutta. Some were so young that they hadn't even finished school. Their parents were understandably horrified. But Teresa found a way out. She didn't give the girls up — they were so much like her in their spontaneous enthusiasm — but she insisted on their graduating; and along with the work in the slums she put them through such intense cramming that they all passed their exams with flying colors.

"Our parents thought that studying was more important than anything else then," one of them recalls. "But Mother said: 'No, no, the sooner you come, the better.' She looked young and very dynamic. She filled us with enthusiasm. So we joined her, first Sister Agnes, then Sister Gertrude and Sister Dorothy. We came in twos or threes at the same time, and formed a group...."

In their first tiny settlement they all slept in the same room, like the proverbial sardines in a can. Then in a crazy way — pious folk would call it a miracle — Teresa came upon the building at 54A Lower Circular Road that still serves as the community's headquarters today. A well-to-do Muslim was emigrating to Pakistan and, out of sympathy for socially committed Catholics, he sold his three-story house for a song to the archdiocese of Calcutta.

The girls who had dropped out of their bourgeois families put on the white sari of the poor; and in 1950 the new order was founded under the name of the Bearers of Christ's Love in the Slums. They have since become better known as the Missionaries of Charity.

A Life-Threatening Friendship

The Indian women who first made up the group were joined by sisters from Europe, America, and Africa. Those who wished to come aboard didn't have to bring much with them — physical and mental health, common sense, and a robust sense of humor. Yet they had, and have, the strength to endure all their lives under conditions that are often extremely harsh.

The sisters arise at 5:30 in the morning. As is the custom in monasteries and other religious communities, breakfast doesn't come till after private prayer, Mass, and a few daily chores. They then leave the house more or less merrily to work in schools, clinics, and hospices. In principle they always travel in pairs, as the streetwise Mother Teresa stipulated: "In an emergency two heads are better than one, and four hands can do more than two."

The continuous stress of their lives is interrupted only by a prayer session in the afternoon and a silent hour of adoration in the evening. "Otherwise it would be impossible to work," is Sister Agnes's explanation for the close interweaving of action and contemplation. "You have to be spiritually motivated."

Candidates from a "better background" are especially liable to find the atmosphere of poverty in the houses more burdensome than the often monotonous work and the rigid daily schedule. "We want to live just as the poor do," the sisters say, "so that we really sense how they feel. There's a big difference between working for the poor while you're living in quite acceptable conditions and working for them while being very poor yourself, the way we do. It's much harder, but it's also wonderful."

In addition to the three familiar promises of poverty, chastity, and obedience, on the day of her final vows every Sister of Charity also takes a special fourth vow, as a gift to God: she promises lifelong, exclusive commitment to the poor and the renunciation of all material rewards. In practice this is fiercely difficult, but as Mother Teresa (who was supposed to be so naive about social and political issues) kept insisting, the refusal to work for the rich gives the sisters an enormous freedom. There are no compromising dependencies, no interference by generous donors in their service.

The Missionaries by no means rely solely on their kind hearts. As a matter of policy they all learn a profession, so as to provide effective help for the poor as nurses, teachers, or social workers. Some study medicine; some go into law, to represent the interests of the exploited. Meanwhile they run hospitals and rehabilitation centers for lepers, mobile clinics, pharmacies, homes for handicapped children and single mothers, shelters for the homeless, alcoholics, drug addicts, people with AIDS and TB, abandoned infants and toddlers. The sisters can be found in prisons and Sunday schools. They offer preschool programs and health care in the villages. They organize sewing courses and Bible study groups; they provide warm meals and clothing for slum-dwellers.

What may have begun with a vague feeling of pity soon turns into a very hard job, exhausting and sometimes even life-threatening. One day at Mother Teresa's Shishu Bhavan Center in Calcutta the food supplies had run out, and a constantly growing crowd waited in vain for their accustomed warm meal. Suddenly a handful of desperate, starving rowdies attacked the sisters and tried to set fire to the house. Another time not far from Calcutta some lepers, dissatisfied with their poor accommodations, seized a couple of Missionaries, locked them inside a panel truck, and started pushing it toward a canal. The police just managed to save the sisters from drowning.

Teresa herself was more than once the target of massive threats from, among others, furious Hindus when she opened her first hospice and, at the very beginning of her work, from bands of adolescents who regularly used to mob the entrance to her settlement. Finally she went out all by herself, one tough little woman, and faced them down: "Come on, just kill me, if you want," she hissed. "But stop disturbing our work!" From that point on, we are told, the delinquents became her fans.

In the highland of Darjeeling a powerful landslide destroyed a number of villages and left many people homeless. Teresa immediately got into a jeep and drove to the disaster area. At a sharp curve on the road through the pass a truck came barreling toward her. Her head struck against the windshield and she suffered severe lacerations. "A little deeper, and she would have lost an eye," recalls one of her companions.

It's risky being a friend of the poor.

Mother Teresa with sisters from her community.

He has chosen us. We didn't choose him first. Still we should respond by making our congregation something beautiful — something really beautiful — for God. For this we have to give everything, whatever we can. We should cling to Jesus, press around him, seize hold of him, and never let him get away for anything in the world. We have to fall in love with him. Our special mission consists in working for the salvation and sanctification of the poorest, not just in the shantytowns, but all over the world, wherever they may be:

- *by living the love of God in prayer and service, in a life marked by the simplicity and humility of the Gospel;*

- *by loving the presence of Jesus in the form of bread;*

- *by serving him in the wretched disguise of the materially and mentally poorest of the poor, by recognizing and reviving in them the image of God and their lost resemblance to him. . . .*

We are called "Missionaries of Charity."

A missionary is sent with the charge of proclaiming a message. Just as Jesus was sent by his Father, we too have been sent by him. We have been filled with his Spirit, to be witnesses to his Gospel of love and compassion: first in our communities, then in the domain of our apostolate, among the poorest of the poor throughout the world.

As Missionaries we should be:

- *bearers of the love of God, ready, like Mary, to set out hastily in search of souls;*

- *burning lamps to enlighten all people;*

- *the salt of the earth;*

- *souls consumed by only one longing: Jesus.*

We should constantly guard these principles in our mind and heart and thus bring the Lord to places where he has never been before.

We should

- *undauntedly do the things that he did: bravely heading into dangers, even taking on death with him and for him; . . .*

- *always be willing to go anywhere in the world, while respecting and appreciating the customs of other peoples, their way of life and their languages; be prepared, so far as necessary, to adapt ourselves;*

- *be happy to take upon ourselves every labor and toil, to make every sacrifice that our missionary life demands.*

The Cry of the Dead Children

Her dearest friends were the smallest, the defenseless ones; Teresa was crazy about children. She would cradle a newborn in her arms with infinite care and show it with a gleam in her eye, as proudly as if she were its mother: "See, there's life in him."

She couldn't understand complaints about the population explosion in India. Children were, after all, "God's life." He made the world rich enough to nourish everyone: "There can never be enough of them!"

Who could be poorer or more helpless than small children? "I see God in their eyes," Teresa always said. Her Missionaries of Charity search the streets for newborns who have been thrown away, babies no one wants, and especially for preemies. They find them on garbage dumps, in the gutters, on the steps of public buildings, at the doors of church institutions.

They have saved the lives of thousands of them in their nurseries. Of course, many have died too, because they weren't viable from the outset. "I believe that some mothers have taken drugs to get rid of the children," says Sister Agnes, the erstwhile frail Bengali girl, about the premature births. "The children have been poisoned and need a great deal of care. But they fight for their lives, and some make it. It's like a miracle. Some weigh less than two pounds. They can't suck and have to be fed through the nose or intravenously till they're strong enough to suck."

Helpful Western friends who wish to send clothes to the nurseries have no idea of the condition these tiny candidates for death are in. Just to be on the safe side, the Missionaries warn them that caps for these babies shouldn't be any larger than a tennis ball.

Sometimes the sisters also pick up bigger girls and boys; or they take one or two children off the hands of an overburdened widow who has five or six and give them a solid preparation in a trade. To illustrate the misery children face in India, Mother

Teresa liked to tell about a little boy whom the sisters brought to her. He was suffering from a bad stomachache because he had apparently eaten some sort of garbage. "So I sat the child down and asked him what he had eaten. That morning? Nothing. Last night? Nothing. Yesterday? Nothing. The pains came from hunger!"

Teresa created an international fund that helps children by financing programs to train them. The sisters bring pregnant unmarried woman to shelters, lovingly care for them until they give birth, and afterward try as best they can to support them with food, clothing, and jobs.

Mother Teresa never tired of defending the right to life of the unborn who bear God's creative power within them: "Life belongs to God, and we have no right to destroy it." Whether the laws of the state legalize abortion or not was a point that left her completely indifferent. She felt strongly that there was no greater sin against creation than abortion: "One doesn't simply kill life, one puts one's own ego above God. Humans decide who shall live and who shall die. They want to turn themselves into Almighty God.... It seems to me you can hear the cry of the children who have been murdered, a cry that echoes before the throne of God!"

In 1988, shortly before the Berlin Wall came down, Teresa visited her two settlements in East Germany, where a very liberal abortion law was in effect and where every year an estimated eighty thousand pregnancies were terminated. In an overflowing St. Hedwig's Cathedral in East Berlin she led the way in founding a home for pregnant women in desperate straits and suggested that every abortion meant a double death: the killing of the child — and the killing of one's own conscience.

Back home in India she protested against the sterilization campaigns by the government (which in rural districts with overzealous bureaucrats often led to compulsory sterilizations and dealt Indira Gandhi a crushing electoral defeat) and fought against the discrimination directed at the girls and women raped by soldiers in the civil war in Bangladesh; for the children born of those rapes she immediately opened a home.

Family Planning Instead of Abortion

If you want to have a child, then you should have one, Teresa used to say. "But if you prefer not to have it, don't kill it — give it to me!" Still, she never delivered the sort of damning judgments popular in strict Catholic circles on women who have abortions. Once when a young woman came to her in tears and told her she couldn't get over an abortion she had had years before, Teresa took her hands and said: "Take care of a child that's as old as yours would have been now, and look on every future child you have as a gift."

Mother Teresa always talked about family planning, her co-workers jest, but she never practiced it herself: she was always getting more children. As a matter of fact, she did talk a lot about natural methods of contraception. In the hunger-ridden lands of the Third World, she said, limiting the number of children is obviously needed — but the individual's freedom of decision had to be respected, and the path chosen had to be a "natural" one, controlling reproduction without destroying life. "Self-discipline out of love for one another," she called it, when poor women learn to count the days in their menstrual cycle (which the sisters teach them to do with beads) and to take their basal body temperature.

Teresa's campaigns, supported by the Indian Bishops Conference, to popularize "natural family planning" have been quite successful: in a single year, as the authorities gratefully determined, the population growth in Calcutta dropped by more than thirty thousand births.

But for the girls and women whom nevertheless find themselves carrying an unwanted child — and that keeps happening a thousand times over — she offered adoption as an alternative to abortion: "Don't kill it, give it to me!"

Her practice of arranging adoptions outside of India was not without its critics. Indian newspapers ran a campaign against the "sale of Indian children." Needless to say, Mother Teresa never took money for this, and she never felt any sort of resentment against the country. She simply wanted "her children" to have a chance for humane care and a decent education.

To be sure, clever people sometimes pretend to offer help in hopes of acquiring a cheap messenger boy from among the sisters' charges. But the Missionaries keep a watchful eye out. Sister Agnes gets angry at such people, "because they want to get a poor person to do the work for two or three. When I ask them what they intend to pay, they duck the question. . . . Sometimes they say 'forty or fifty rupees,' and I ask them, 'Would *you* work for that much?' . . . Then people come and tell me, 'Sister, times are very hard; we can't afford to give the messengers much.' So I tell them, 'Then you can do without a messenger. Hard times for you are hard times for the poor too.'"

3

"Let Them Go Home with a Smile"

The Goddess Kali's Home for the Dying

You pick up the dying from the streets
and carry them into heaven.

— A Hindu

"Nowadays when we tell the other sisters how we used to live in the first group, they can't believe it," Sister Bernard observes. When she had Teresa as a teacher in St. Mary's High School, she was still called Beatrice Rozario. A few years later she joined the Missionaries of Charity, to the horror of her family.

To this day the younger sisters are stunned to hear Sister Bernard's account of the congregation's miserable beginnings: "They say it's incredible. It *was* incredible! It had to be that way."

"We always had to go begging for medications," she reports. "Mother begged from the different missions, from friends, from everyone. Now at least she gets contributions; back then she was unknown. She practically lived on the street herself. She used to go begging from door to door; and there were people who simply turned their back on her. But God helped us. It came. Something always turned up. . . . We had to get by with the bare minimum. . . . We used the cheapest soap we could get. We thought powdered detergents were for rich people. Think about it, most of us were studying at the high school back then. Our congregation hadn't been founded. . . . It was hard. But she didn't want to have it easy....She was constantly on her feet and working away."

"She" — Mother Teresa — was not yet forty, and fantastically dynamic. She proudly wrote to a friend in Europe that she already had three zealous coworkers and was active in five slums. "What need and what longing for God! And yet there are only a couple of us who bring the Lord to them. You should see their expectant faces, the glow in their eyes when they see the sisters come.... Ask our dear Lady to send us still more sisters. Even if there were twenty of us, we would all have our hands full just in Calcutta."

Another letter from two years later: "Oh, there's so awfully much to do. Now we are five in all. But if it pleases God there will be more. Then we will be able to form a true ring of charity in Calcutta, and from our centers in the various slums the love of the Lord can shine unimpeded through this metropolis of Calcutta."

A few more years passed, and Teresa's sisters were going to Ranchi and Jhansi, to Coimbatore and Andra Pradesh and finally to the capital of Delhi, where they got in touch with the authorities responsible for social programs and financing, and where Prime Minister Nehru himself dedicated Teresa's new home for children.

"Would you like me to show you our work?" she asked him. "No, Mother," Nehru answered. "I know it. That's why I came."

Meanwhile Teresa had drawn up a rule for her community, a program of consistent poverty — so radical that Rome felt it had to smooth out and correct various passages before officially approving the regulations. For example, she had pressed the renunciation of possessions so far that the order wouldn't even own its own settlements. Francis of Assisi had once had similar plans — and he was no more successful than Teresa in pushing them through. She had wanted to sign over the order's houses to the Vatican, but that would have led to legal chaos, since in India the Vatican is considered a foreign corporation.

Nobody, of course, dared infringe upon the basic approach that Teresa formulated in her draft: "It is our goal to satisfy our Lord Jesus Christ's insatiable longing for love . . . through free and undivided service to the poorest of the poor."

Teresa never regretted her decision. Once she made up her mind to leave her family and become a nun, through all the following decades she "never doubted for a second that I had done the right thing," she declared in an interview. And why not? "It was God's will. It was *his* choice. . . . I was sure back then, and I'm still convinced today, that he's the one [who made the choice] and not I."

The Congregation of the Missionaries of Charity is only a small instrument in the hands of God. We must take care that it stays that way, a little instrument. Very often I feel like a little pen in his hands. He's the one who thinks, writes, and acts; I am to be just a pencil, nothing more.

- *You have been sent, you haven't picked out the place where you are going. You have been sent, exactly as Jesus was sent to us.*

- *You haven't been sent to teach, but to learn: learn to be meek and humble of heart. This is just what Jesus has demanded of us: "Learn from me; for I am gentle and lowly in heart."*

- *You have been sent to serve and not to be served: serve with a humble heart! Don't avoid strenuous work. Always be ready to be the first one to do it.*

- *Be a source of joy in your community.*

After receiving the Pope John XXIII Peace Prize.

- *Go to the poor with zeal and joy.*

- *Make haste to serve as Mary did.*

- *Choose the hardest things. Go forth with a humble and generous heart. Don't set out with ideas that are at odds with your way of life: with lofty theological principles about what you would like to teach. Rather go to learn and serve.*

- *Share what you have received with a humble heart.*

- *Go to the poor with great tenderness. Serve them with tender, sympathetic love.*

- *Say yes to peace. . . . Hold your tongue rather than saying a word that might wound someone.*

- *Dedicate yourself without reservations. Give of your self generously, unconditionally.*

"They Take Better Care of Their Dogs!"

Desmond Doig of the *Statesman* — something like the *Times* of India — was the first journalist to write about Mother Teresa. He did so because he had never met a person with so much energy. "I saw her," he says, "occupying land, taking over a building, and setting up shop where, as they say, angels would have feared to tread, because she was convinced that it was necessary for 'her people' and for her work."

But outside of India people didn't begin to talk about Teresa and her sisters until word got around about her commitment to the dying. Spoon-feeding undernourished children, bringing rice and bread to the poor — there seemed to be nothing special about that. But building homes in a hopelessly overpopulated country for people who were doomed to die anyway, who had only a matter of hours to live . . . ?

Nowhere else did Teresa's unconditional appreciation for every human life, no matter how wretched, collide so painfully with bourgeois values as it did here.

Michael Gomes, the man who provided Teresa with her first modest accommodations in Calcutta, reports about the origin of these homes for the dying: one day a dying man was found on the street right next to Campbell Hospital. Mother Teresa tried in vain to get him admitted. When she returned from the pharmacy with some medications, the man lay dead on the sidewalk. Teresa reacted with consternation and fury: "They take better care of their dogs and cats than of their human brothers and sisters. They would never allow their pets to die this way!"

She filed a complaint at the police commissioner's office and then began to reflect on what she herself could do about these conditions. The dead man by the side of the road was no isolated case. Every morning crews would go around the streets of Calcutta collecting the dead bodies on carts. It was an everyday sanitary procedure like garbage collection elsewhere in the world.

The story of the fight against anonymous death got off to a start that was as moving as it was embarrassing: the paupers from the slums of Moti Jheel collected money to found a house for the dying. They gave it the poetic name of Nirmal Hriday, "the Place of the Pure Heart." But what did "house" mean here? The tiny hospice had only two beds, and it soon had to be closed because the neighbors rebelled. They were afraid of the smell of death.

For months on end the stubborn nun went looking for places for terminally ill and dying people. She tried the authorities; she looked in the hospitals and nursing homes — in vain. What doctors or other care-givers would scramble to get patients, most of whom were just about to die? In those years after the partition of the country Calcutta had to deal with two million refugees from the newly created country of Pakistan. Besides, starvation in the countryside was driving masses of people to the city.

So it was a hopeless undertaking, given all that chaos, to try to awaken interest in dying slum-dwellers. Didn't every corpse mean one less problem?

But in the city's health department there was an official who evidently took a different view. One day he led Teresa to the temple of the goddess Kali in the throbbing center of Calcutta, where a *dormashalah* (shelter for Hindu pilgrims), no longer in service, lay empty. That is, hoboes and crooks had taken over the dormitories and held wild binges there.

Nevertheless, Teresa was enthusiastic: pious Hindus, when they felt their last hour coming, were accustomed to seeking out the temple of Kali, the goddess of death, to die and be cremated in a holy place. The site seemed ideal for a hospice. The sisters needed twenty-four hours to fix up the building and to install their "patients" on simple cots.

Birthday Celebration with Hindus and Buddhists

Calcutta was not a scene of unmitigated joy over the activities of *Mataji,* "mother," as Teresa was tenderly called by the poor. The four hundred priests from the temple complex viewed the novel use of the venerable old pilgrim shelter with mixed feelings. Rumors claimed that the only reason this foreign woman took elderly Hindus into her home for the dying was to convert them. This was a deliberate lie, because from the beginning the Missionaries had left any preaching to the priests and had always treated non-Christian religions with respect.

One skeptical journalist watched with astonishment as a co-worker of Mother Teresa's moistened the lips of a dying Hindu with water from the sacred Ganges. This was completely understandable, Teresa told him, because in her houses every dying person was given every consolation of his or her own faith that he or she requested. Muslim burials and Hindu cremations were carried out in strict accordance with tradition. And the babies picked up on the street were not baptized until they had gotten big enough to be able to make their own decisions.

"There is only one God," Mother Teresa explained in her simple way, "and he is the God of everyone. So it's important that all men and women be looked upon as equal in the sight of God. I have always said that we should help a Hindu become a better Hindu, a Muslim become a better Muslim, and a Catholic become a better Catholic."

"Let us pray to our common Father," was her invitation, whenever she got together with adherents of different religious communities. In her leprosarium in Titagarh, which has about five hundred patients, "Thirty families are Catholic; and the rest are Hindus, Muslims, or Sikhs," says the director, Brother Vinod. "But they all come to our devotions. Around 7:00 P.M. they all gather for half an hour. And we read from the Bible or other Scriptures; they can read from any book they want. Sometimes a patient gives a little talk."

On the twenty-fifth anniversary of her community the woman whom some dismissed as an obdurate traditionalist celebrated the event with prayers in churches, synagogues, and temples, together with Anglicans, Baptists, Jews, Armenians, Parsees, Hindus, Sikhs, Jains, and Buddhists.

This has nothing whatsoever to do with some sort of laid-back/anything-goes piety, indifferent to the truth. Teresa always was a fervent Catholic. With every fiber of her being she clung to the traditions in which she grew up. But it was also clear to her that "God works in his own way in the hearts of human beings; and we can't know how close they are to him. But we will always know from their actions whether they are at his disposal or not. Whether Hindu, Muslim, or Christian, how you live your

life proves whether or not you belong completely to him. We may
not judge or condemn. . . . The only thing that counts is that we
love."

The Woman Who Stood Up the Pope

For a while things looked bad for Teresa's first hospice. A police
commissioner showed up in the home for the dying to arrange
the expulsion of the sisters. He was startled to see how Teresa
treated a man's open wounds that were crawling with maggots.
He later told the people who had brought charges against her: "I
am not going to take this lady away from here until your mothers
and sisters come and do her job!"

A priest from the Kali sanctuary likewise came out of mistrust and went away admitting, "I have been serving the goddess
Kali in her temple for thirty years. Today I have seen the Holy
Mother in human form." It didn't take long before the sisters
had won over the Hindu priests and turned them into friends
and comrades-in-arms.

Before long, Hindus who were offering sacrifices on feast days
would make side-trips to bring food to the home for the dying. "I
know what you do here," one of them told the sisters. "You pick
up the dying from the streets and carry them into heaven."

Within a few years there were more than thirty such homes
for the dying all over India. The first one in Calcutta, as we have
seen, was named Nirmal Hriday, "place of the pure heart." For
Teresa it was no meaningless effort to provide a dying person
with a few hours or days of human attention, a little warmth,
or possibly just a smile. "They have lived like beasts," she said.
"At least they ought to die like human beings."

At the end of their lives, Teresa thought, the people collected
off the misery-racked streets should learn that they are human,
that they count, that they are loved by God and cherished by the

women in saris. "We help the poor," Teresa said simply, "to die in peace with God." That was enough.

The sisters gather up the bodies that have been lying in filth somewhere, sometimes already partly eaten by ants or rats, and place them in rickshas or vans. At other times city ambulances bring in the patients that no hospital will accept. Of those who, thanks to the good care they've gotten, manage to leave the hospice alive, only a few get completely better and, if they are lucky, find work. The sisters try to accommodate the others in homes.

Every one of these poor wretches, it seems, was worth more to Mother Teresa than the whole world. When Pope Paul VI visited India in 1964, he was escorted in triumph through the streets of Bombay — in a white Lincoln Continental that he had been given by American Catholics. The pope used this luxury car only once — he preferred a jeep anyway — and donated it to Mother Teresa. At the first opportunity she raffled it off and raised around $100,000 for the poor.

But when the Holy Father wanted to hand over his gift, Mother Teresa wasn't there. She had gone off to be with a dying man by the name of Onil. She held his emaciated hands and encouraged him. And before Onil passed on into a land without pain, he said quietly: "I have lived like an animal on the street, but now I can die like an angel...."

The "Exhilarating" Atmosphere of Death

It may be that even in the developed countries of the West dying people want to have a Mother Teresa at their side. Their misery has another face, but it calls out in the same way for imaginative

In a refugee camp.

love. Under the pretext of providing them with the best medical care available terminally ill people are thrust out of their familiar environment, hooked up to machines, and impeccably monitored. They long for encouragement and intimacy, for someone to hold their hand and listen to them — but instead they are left alone with their guilt, anxiety, and fearful expectations.

The paralyzing fear of death in our affluent society, obsessed with youth and achievement but humanly impoverished as it is, denies dignity to the act of dying and comfort to the person who dies. In the face of such mechanisms of repression and exclusion Teresa preached a very simple message: "Death is nothing more than a continuation of life, its fulfillment. . . . Those who believe it is the end fear death. If one could convince people that death is no more than going home to God, there would be no more fear."

In the Christian culture of the late Middle Ages this was known as the *ars moriendi,* the art of integrating death into life, thereby preserving the dignity of death and avoiding the banalization of life. Mistrustful observers like journalist Desmond Doig from the *Statesman* have continually marveled at the atmosphere of silent peace in Teresa's homes for the dying. They have even spoken of an "exhilarating," "cheerful" mood, without bitterness or despair. Doig notes that for him death was always like the closing of a book, like the withering of a flower; and he confesses that in Nirmal Hriday he sensed something unique: "Perhaps it was just the absence of fear, which might in itself be a first sign of faith."

In the middle of one of the countless interviews that she gave, Teresa suddenly stopped to listen to herself, as if from far away, and began to whisper. "Just let them experience this one happiness," she prayed her heavenly friend, who bursts open the graves. "In their last moment let them wipe away their trouble with a last smile."

She recalled a dreadful call from New Delhi: on a garbage heap they had found a woman covered from head to toe with wounds, burning with fever and with only a few days to live. "She cried and cried, even after we had washed her and put her to bed. Finally she said: 'I'm not crying because I'm going to die. It's not that. It's because it was my son who threw me away there!'"

Day after day Teresa spoke with her. What her son had done to his mother once she became a useless burden was terrible. But he was her flesh and blood; he would regret the deed — surely he had been in a state of confusion at the time. "Be a mother to him," Teresa urged. "Forgive him!"

For a long time the deathly sick woman wasn't capable of that. But just as she was getting ready to pass on to another life, she said in a weak voice: "I forgive him, my God, I forgive him" — and died in the arms of Mother Teresa. In peace.

One day in Calcutta a man came to us with a prescription. He said: "My only child is dying. The medicine he needs can't be gotten in India; you have to import it from abroad." As we were still speaking with one another, a man came in with a basket full of medications. On top of the pile lay the medicine we were looking for. Had the man come before or afterward, I wouldn't have seen it. But just at that time God, in his tender love, among all the millions and tens of millions of children, was so concerned for this little child in the slums of Calcutta that he sent the medicine at the right moment, to save the child. I praise the tenderness and love of God, because every child, whether from a poor or rich family, is a child of God, made by the Creator of all things.

4

"They Are the Wounds of Christ"

Leprosy Means Being Buried Alive

Teresa the skilled organizer ("I never think about money, it just keeps coming") raffled off the pope's Lincoln for five times its value. With the profits she built Shanti Nagar, the city of peace, near Calcutta, a rehabilitation center for lepers, of whom there were three million in India and more than fifty thousand in the region of Calcutta alone. The Missionaries of Charity take care of them and give those that have been cured vocational training, so that they don't have to beg anymore.

It all began with five lepers who had lost their jobs and homes and who turned in despair to Mother Teresa because they were hungry. She understood immediately, and a new field of work opened up for her sisters: boundless, exhausting, thankless — just the way she liked it.

An idealistic young doctor (who happened to be a specialist in leprosy) joined the community; and he was able to give the sisters a thorough schooling. Teresa had two ambulances she had been given refitted as mobile clinics and sent them through the slums along with medications and advisory teams.

The work of education was especially important. People had to learn that leprosy isn't a punishment for sin, that it's curable with timely intervention, using simple, cheap methods. These call for baths, massage, kinetic therapy, and a mixture of drugs costing around $20 that completely eradicate the disease in a maximum of three years. To exclude the danger of infection generally requires no more than a brief hospital stay combined with intensive drug therapy.

But often enough family members and neighbors of lepers panic and condemn the victims to an existence that is no better than being buried alive: they are locked up in back rooms and sheds or immediately thrown out of the house. Sometimes they are left exposed to the elements in wild mountainous areas or walled into rocky caves. "Among the lepers," Teresa explained, "there are many educated persons, many rich and capable people. But because of the disease their relatives have driven them from their houses; and very often their own children don't want to see them anymore.... Now they live in the slums, unknown, unloved, and uncared for."

One high official in the municipal government of Calcutta didn't like the sisters at all. He thought the order was a publicity trick by European Christians to win Hindus for the church. Then he got leprosy. His family put him out on the street. The Missionaries nursed him back to health; and he repaid them by using his talents to speak out for the lepers and toiling away as an administrator of Shanti Nagar.

A City on Stilts

Not quite thirty years after beginning their work among the lepers the sisters were already maintaining 122 leprosy centers and 11 rehabilitation clinics in India, where a total of 163,000 lepers received help. One of the first centers was Titagarh in Calcutta's industrial zone: a collection of huts (imaginatively cobbled together out of jute, bamboo, tin, and tiles), some of them propped up on stakes on a piece of abandoned land right next to a railway embankment.

"This is uninhabited land; it belongs to the railroad," Sister Bernard proudly informs visitors from abroad. "In the beginning we simply squatted on it and began to spread out along the tracks. We hope to create a colony where families of lepers can build their own houses and plow their own fields."

Meanwhile the number of such adventurous stopgap arrangements as Titagarh has swelled; most have been tremendously successful. The village of cockeyed huts on the embankment has turned into the Gandhi Prem Nivas leper settlement, with solid houses, all painted in bright, cheerful colors, with clinics, work places, residential homes, a school, and ponds for drinking water. On average fourteen hundred patients are treated here every month. Many lepers who have been cured stay on to work as nurses or instructors, because learning a good profession — a trade that makes one as independent as possible from the fickle kindness of one's fellows — is a matter of life and death for the patients. Wonder drugs by no means erase the leprous "mark of Cain" on the forehead of its victims. German leprosy specialist Dr. Ruth Pfau and her assistants watched in horror as their patients ripped open their healing wounds just so they wouldn't be released from the safe confines of the clinic. And many former patients returned in discouragement to the hospital because no one would hire them. It's obvious that rehabilitation and reintegration into society are just as important as medical treatment.

In the beginning the sisters limited themselves to a little bit of "occupational therapy": the patients wove their own bandages and learned to make pouches to hold their medicines. Carpentry and shoe repair workshops, brickworks and vegetable gardens in the leprosy centers ensured the maintenance of the inhabitants. Their own rice paddies and wheat fields made them self-sufficient. At the very beginning of Shanti Nagar Teresa got hold of an old printing press, so that the lepers could print up brochures and a newspaper, could take part in life once more and earn some money.

Today the training programs aim at preparing the patients for an independent existence after their release: they often begin their new lives with a loom or a sewing machine. If they still have some money or if the sisters can drum up credit, they start little businesses for themselves.

It's quite possible they never would have managed all this if the Missionaries hadn't helped them to rediscover their self-respect, the knowledge of their own dignity. The patients, Sister Bernard declares, are often fantastic. "And we learn a lot from them. Do you know what they say sometimes? 'We have leprosy outside, on our bodies, but not in our hearts.'"

Father Henry, one of Mother Teresa's first coworkers, can recall no more beautiful Christmas than the one at the beginning of his assignment there. The Christian lepers had built a little church in a slum called Belgachia between a garbage dump and an open sewer. "What a Mass that was! The lepers who couldn't move by themselves were carried by the others. It was really tremendous."

"We See Jesus in the Broken Bodies of the Poor"

It often happens that, as a result of working constantly with severe cases of leprosy, one of the sisters becomes infected herself and has to undergo treatment. The nuns who come down with leprosy view this as a stroke of good fortune. They are proud to have been allowed to share the distress of their patients to the point of physical pain. Teresa's sisters, it's easy to forget, don't simply visit wretched poverty; they want to share it. In the dirt-covered, dying man or woman on the edge of the road, in the leper with his rotting limbs, in the cancer patient whose body is one open wound, they find Christ, the center of their life. To them that isn't just a fine phrase, but a potent reality; otherwise they couldn't endure their existence in hell. Above all they couldn't smile and radiate kindness as they work.

"When you handle the sores and wounds of the poor," Teresa always impressed on her novices, "you must never forget that they are the wounds of Christ." That is why divine worship and social commitment fit together so seamlessly for these Gospel activists.

The workday begins with the celebration of the Eucharist; and as they go out on the streets to gather the dying, or keep their watch at deathbeds, they know that this is a continuation of their morning worship — only in another form. "In holy communion," Mother Teresa explained, "we have Christ in the form of bread. In our work we find him in the form of flesh and blood. It's the same Christ. 'I was hungry, I was naked, I was sick, I was homeless.'"

"It's the same Christ": Teresa always preached this equation (which she based on Jesus' "Judgment speech" in Matthew 25) with a sacred seriousness. This sentence is the key to the life of the sisters, the guarantee that they really are concerned with others, that they aren't looking for the satisfaction one gets from doing good deeds or appeasing a guilty conscience.

Teresa once said that if she didn't know that it was the body of Christ, no force in the world could move her to take hold of a body eaten up by worms. But for her it was actually quite simple: "If we can see Jesus in the form of bread, we can also see him in the broken bodies of the poor."

"We put that immediately into practice," is how she accounted for this experience. A person deprived of the happiness of faith will probably never be able to understand her.

"We need the poor so as to touch *him*. We find strength and nourishment in the Eucharist; and if we have been strengthened, we want to use this strength, to pass it on. That is why you always see the sisters running: they never walk. We're called the 'running congregation'!"

"We all yearn for eternal bliss with God," she continues, "but it lies in our power to experience this bliss here and now — to

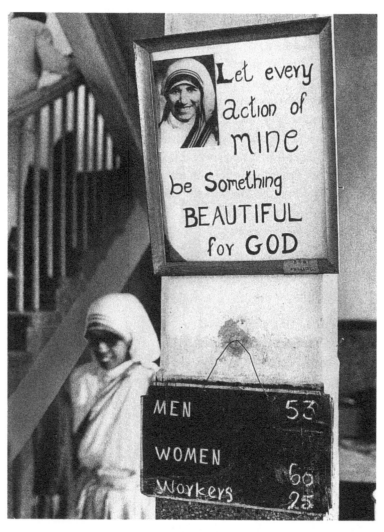

Home for the dying in Calcutta, whose halls used to belong to the adjoining Hindu temple.

be happy with God at this very moment. Being happy with him now means loving as he loves, helping as he helps, giving as he gives, serving as he serves, saving as he saves, being with him twenty-four hours a day, touching him in his pitiful disguise."

That is why the sisters' work schedule, for all its stress, has room even on the worst days for a full hour of adoration. That is why every visitor to her settlements is led first to the chapel to greet the "master of the house." And why Teresa, who begged all over the world for financial aid for her poor, never hesitated an instant about setting aside several hundred pounds sterling from donations to buy a beautiful chalice for the new novitiate. That way, to her mind, the kindhearted donors would be daily close to Christ, on the altar.

Who is Jesus for me?

Jesus is the Word made "Flesh."
Jesus is the Bread of Life.
Jesus is the Sacrificial Lamb — offered for our sins on the cross.
Jesus is the victim offered at holy Mass for the sins of the world and for my sins.
Jesus is the word that must be spoken.
Jesus is the truth that must be proclaimed.
Jesus is the light that should shine out.
Jesus is the life that should be lived.
Jesus is the love that we should love.
Jesus is the joy that we should dispense.
Jesus is the peace that we should give.
Jesus is the Bread of Life to be eaten.
Jesus is the hungry one, whom we are to feed.
Jesus is the thirsty one, whom we are to give drink.
Jesus is the naked one, whom we are to clothe.

Jesus is the homeless one, whom we are to welcome in.
Jesus is the sick one, whom we are to heal.
Jesus is the lonely one, whom we are to love.
Jesus is the unwanted one, whom we are to accept.
Jesus is the leper, whose wounds we are to wash.
Jesus is the beggar, to whom we are to give a smile.
Jesus is the drunkard, to whom we are to listen.
Jesus is the handicapped, whom we are to protect.
Jesus is the little child, whom we are to embrace.
Jesus is the blind man, whom we are to lead.
Jesus is the cripple, with whom we are to walk.
Jesus is the drug addict, whom we are to befriend.
Jesus is the prostitute, whom we are to save from danger and
*   with whom we are to be friends.*
Jesus is the prisoner, whom we are to visit.
Jesus is the old man or woman, whom we are to serve.
For me
Jesus is my God.
Jesus is my bridegroom.
Jesus is my life.
Jesus is my only love.
Jesus is my all in all.
Jesus is my one and all.
Jesus, I love you with my whole heart, with my whole being.

I have given him everything, even my sins, and he has taken me to be
his bride in tenderness and love. Now and for my whole life I am the
bride of my crucified bridegroom. Amen.

Does one's fellow human being ultimately vanish here behind a
pious fiction? Doesn't the needy neighbor merge so powerfully
with Christ that he or she loses all individuality and becomes

a mere test case for the power of the helper's faith? These are legitimate questions. But anyone who has actually seen how personally and attentively the Missionaries deal with their patients, and what warm human relations grow up between them, will quickly put such fears to rest.

Perhaps this matter-of-course identification of every suffering person with Christ is also the best guarantee that help and care won't depend on the appeal or good behavior of those being helped. In a prayer composed for her coworkers Teresa asked for a "seeing faith," which recognizes the crucified Lord "in the unhandsome disguise of the irritating, the demanding, and the unreasonable": "Then my work never gets boring."

Could this realistic judge of people ever have been called naive?

5

"Once You Have God within You, Then It's for Life"

Crazy Charity between Laughter and Despair

Some of God's universal love has rubbed off on Mother Teresa.
— Malcolm Muggeridge

One wonders where the improbable energy of this slight, skinny woman, always slightly bent over as she walked, came from. She spoke softly and artlessly about prayer, the poor, and the good Lord, but even when addressing university audiences and international organizations she could always count on spellbound attention.

She was anything but a radiant presence; and yet the great ones of the world — you could see this on television — became silent and embarrassed when they looked into her wrinkled, leathery face, a strikingly good face with its penetrating eyes and serious lips.

Even in grand public scenes, at receptions and prize ceremonies, she remained the simple woman in a sari, always a little bit lost amid a jubilant public. But she was seldom shy; she was self-possessed without a trace of ostentatiousness. In her coarse sandals she would climb up on the speaker's platform, with a threadbare wool vest over her white sari.

At the 1978 German Catholic Congress in Freiburg prominent guests bowed and scraped around this by-now legendary

little woman from Calcutta. At lunch in the Collegium Bor-
romäum, Federal President Walter Scheel, Prime Minister of the
Rhineland/Palatinate and future chancellor Helmut Kohl, Apos-
tolic Nuncio Guido del Mestri (a compatriot of Teresa's), and the
archbishop of Freiburg, Oskar Saier, all sunned themselves alongside her. But after the meal, when everybody got up, Mother
Teresa bolted to the kitchen for an animated chat with the Yugoslavian help, thanking them for their efforts on behalf of the
distinguished company.

She never courted the favor of the mighty; she could afford to express uncomfortable truths, as she did in 1982 at the
show of solidarity for the Third World by the State of Baden-
Würtemberg: at the government villa she attacked the German
policy on refugees, unabashedly challenging Christian Demo-
cratic Prime Minister Lothar Späth: "Open the door, and God
will bless you!"

She often nonplused her interlocutors with her replies. After
watching her attend to a stinking gangrenous wound, an American journalist confessed, "I wouldn't do that for a million
dollars!" "I wouldn't either," she shot back. She was doing it
for God.

"This Half-Smile"

When the highly respected English journalist Malcolm Muggeridge (formerly the editor of Punch, later with the Guardian
and the Daily Telegraph) held his first TV interview with her,
he met a shy, awkward, and above all nonprofessional conversation partner. Teresa sat hunkered down in the BBC studio
saying her rosary, unaware that half the English TV audience
was looking in.

But after her first clumsy answers to the interviewer's questions, she suddenly took control of the discussion and began to

At the Catholic Congress in Freiburg.

speak out frankly. Muggeridge, the media star, put aside his notes and just listened. And the program, which was so technically botched that it shouldn't even have been broadcast to begin with, turned out to have more resonance than any comparable show before or since. Countless letters and contributions poured into the studio. People called nonstop, all saying the same thing: "This woman thrilled me; how can I help her?"

Teresa never became an icon, a remote saintly figure, as some critics kept asserting. She was credible not because she always communicated some kind of blissful peace, but because she was so human.

Muggeridge raved about her "half-smile, at once mocking and enchanting" — a smile with which she could both come close to people *and* maintain an intimate space that belonged to her alone.

She remained the self-willed, unruly little girl she had always been, as her brother, Lazar, said. (On the other hand, he vouched that she had the discipline of an army officer: "You could have come from the military academy.") In the last years of her life she fell seriously ill again and again, but stubbornly forbade her sisters to call a doctor. When her worried companions finally did drag in a physician, she would chat amiably with the good man. But scarcely had he left than she would shred the prescription or hide it under the mattress. And that was how she got better — or at least strong enough to dive back into her work.

One of her schools in Calcutta had hired as a dance teacher a fantastic *manipuri* dancer. In India classical dance is considered a demanding cultural subject like piano or violin instruction in the West. Teresa, of course, thoroughly disapproved of this expensive innovation. The school only ran half-day sessions — why offer such an unusual extra subject?

On the anniversary of the founding of the congregation, which is a joyful festival for the Missionaries, each of their schools offered its own special contribution; and the dance class too had a chance to perform. Teresa's coworkers, who had disregarded her explicit veto and allowed the dancing to go on, feared a harsh reaction. But she laughed and said it was a lovely presentation, that it was a sin not to develop a God-given talent.

"That was Mother all over," noted a friend of the community who related the story. "She was an enormously practical woman. She made rules and broke them. That was her strength."

"Sometimes I Feel like an Empty Shell"

The weary, bent-down, worn-to-the-bone nun with the calloused hands — this is the image of Mother Teresa that immediately stirs up guilt feelings in observers from the West, as ever the richest part of the world.

The other image is the nun serenely frolicking with her novices, more the big sister than the authoritarian convent superior, a woman who could have a great time laughing at the little weaknesses of her companions — and most of all at her own — while mischievously enjoying her own sharp tongue. In one settlement thieves had filched forty thousand lire, and the sisters felt terrible about it. "Don't worry, it was only money," Mother Teresa told them. "It would have been worse if they had abducted you. But I don't think there's much danger of that; you're not that good-looking. And now off you go, to work!"

How she loved to laugh. She liked to tell the story about the sisters dressed head to toe in white (from a later contemplative branch of her order) who were walking through a park in New York City, saying the rosary. A man ran into them and started crying out in terror: "I'm not ready! I'm not ready!" He thought the sisters were angels specially dispatched from heaven to get him. "That shows you what people expect from us!" Teresa concluded with sudden seriousness, as she reported the grotesque incident.

Mother Teresa with Pope Paul VI.

A German companion of hers was with her in Rome in 1969 when Pope Paul VI accepted the articles of association from the International Community of the Coworkers of Mother Teresa. The next day Teresa suggested having a picnic in the Alban Hills. The whole thing had the atmosphere of a school outing, with Teresa challenging the young sisters to a race and the group singing continuously on the way home.

No one could be more disciplined than this nimble foundress, when that was called for. But she hated to be held to any specific way of acting. She didn't want to settle down for the long run anywhere. "I'm like a Bohemian," she said, "who keeps changing from one job to another till the day he dies."

This was a woman who had spread out her arms and tamed a snorting bull in the slum of Howrah one day as it went storming through the streets. ("Maybe the beast was distracted by her sudden appearance," one eyewitness soberly surmised.) Yet this same woman was happy to kneel motionless as a statue in front of the tabernacle in the house chapel, or to comfort a leper by silently embracing him for a long minute.

She had the gift to focus completely on her conversation partner, to make his or her cares and longings her own. "She had our wavelength," summed up an English helper who had first met her as a student. "Whoever she was speaking with became the most important person in her eyes. It made no difference whether you were the president or a nobody off the street."

Is it in bad taste to say that she simply radiated God's nearness? "Some of God's universal love has rubbed off on Mother Teresa," observed Malcolm Muggeridge, "and gives her a perceptible glow, something radiant. She lives so close to her Lord that she has clinging to her the same magic power that drove the masses in Jerusalem and Galilee to pursue him...." The question of where the little old woman got her tremendous powers gave Muggeridge and his wife so much food for thought that they both later converted to Catholicism.

Needless to say, strong as her faith was, even Mother Teresa went through phases of depression and despair. "There are moments," she confessed, "when I feel like an empty shell, an object with no solidity. I feel so lonely, so miserable."

At such times she must have felt the onslaught of massive doubts about the meaning of her work. "What we do," she confided to Fr. Edward Le Joly, "is at bottom so little." Le Joly served the Missionaries of Charity as spiritual director for twenty years. "They praise us for our activity. But really it's just a drop in the bucket, and it's pointless when you measure it against the infinity of human suffering."

Desmond Doig, already quoted before, once tried to comfort her by pointing out that Christ too had doubted, on the Mount of Olives the night before he died. "No," she told Doig, "there was no doubting; he just felt uncertain for a moment, as a human being. That was natural. The moment of acceptance, the moment of self-surrender, that's certainty. But it can mean death for the person. Certainty comes in the moment of self-surrender.... Once you have God within you, then it's for life. You can have other doubts. But this particular one will never come back."

"But what if the uncertainty remains?" her interlocutor persisted. He never forgot Teresa's reply: "Then it's time to get down on your knees," she said.

People are unreasonable,
illogical and self-centered,
LOVE THEM ANYWAY.

When you do good, they will accuse you
of egoism and ulterior motives.
DO GOOD ANYWAY.

*If you are successful,
you will make false friends and real enemies.*
BE SUCCESSFUL ANYWAY.

*The good that you do
will be forgotten tomorrow.*
DO GOOD ANYWAY.

*Sincerity and openness
make you vulnerable.*
BE SINCERE AND OPEN ANYWAY.

*What you have built up over years of work
can be destroyed.*
BUILD ANYWAY.

*Your help is really needed,
but people may attack you
if you help them.*
HELP THEM ANYWAY.

*Give the world your best,
and it will knock your teeth out.*
GIVE THE WORLD YOUR BEST ANYWAY.

No Time for Pious Talk

She was no icon, always under control and serenely dignified. She could get worked up and furious over the unjust distribution of this world's goods. Malcolm Muggeridge found that she was often restless and anxious as she traveled through the better neighborhoods of Calcutta. "The sight of so many buildings put to different uses when she could have accommodated her poor people in them left her depressed. At one building especially, as I recall, she looked inside with a downright grim expression: it was an extraordinarily ugly, but still large and solid memorial for

Queen Victoria...." That was one she could have put to such good use, Teresa grumbled to herself.

She was completely absorbed in the outrageous distress of the world — without indulging in any false sentimentality. Resolute, sober, with a pragmatic sense of reality, she plunged right in wherever there was anything to do, instead of wasting time on pious talk. Her sisters certainly did see her pray and meditate — even as she arrived perched atop a shaky, sky-high truckload of bags of flour. Someone asked her why she bothered herself with such trips. Because, she answered, if she didn't oversee the food transports, most of it would get stolen.

We have already mentioned her talent for occupying land or stunning the authorities with sudden coups. When the Indian and later some international airlines, out of sympathy for her cause, provided her with free plane tickets, she managed, on one occasion, to send six sisters with a thousand pounds of luggage in linen bags and cardboard boxes up to the check-in counter.

"The staff at first looked at the whole thing in shock. They had never seen anything like it," she recalled in amusement. "Normally they only allow forty pounds of baggage per person. On the other hand, the tickets didn't put any upper limit on baggage. It just said: 'Six nuns and their luggage.' And so we handed them blankets, medicine, food, and so forth — all sorts of things that were needed for our work among the poor.... Imagine the faces of the officials when the sisters with their giant piles of luggage passed through customs. The whole shipment had to go through — it couldn't be held up. That's the advantage of complete poverty and complete dependence on God: you don't have to pay for anything."

"Her activity was fantastic," observed Brother Michael, one of her closest coworkers. "While others were still discussing, she was already right in the middle of the job.... Seeing a need and immediately reacting to it were one and the same thing with her."

At the very beginning when the community was still living

in very cramped circumstances in Calcutta, a woman beggar once came along and asked for help. They had no idea where she could be accommodated. Without hesitation Teresa put the woman in her own bed and improvised a place to sleep elsewhere.

For the Missionaries it wasn't always easy to live with this bundle of energy, with all her spontaneous impulses. "Sister, you're going to southern India," she once announced to one of them. The woman thought she would be moving in the next few months and asked cautiously, "When, Mother Teresa?" "This evening," the "boss" replied, laughing, "with the first train in that direction."

Actually, she *was* in the habit of asking her coworkers for advice, whenever important decisions came up. Teresa kept the last word for herself, but she never pretended to be infallible. Her preference for laconic information didn't mean that she didn't reflect thoroughly before making a decision; it was just her way of commenting on certain questions.

"Tomorrow hasn't come yet, and yesterday is over; we live today," she used to explain when asked for the thousandth time about her plans for the future. She sent one American tourist, who was eager to get acquainted with her, to work in one of her homes for the dying. The next day when he asked about her again, he got the same order. But, he complained, he had already *been* in the home the day before. "So?" Teresa replied. "Let him go again. The poor are still there."

Interest in the Third World on the part of Western countries sometimes has more to do with the charm of the exotic than with realistic insights into the need to change unjust social structures. And so she liked to dampen the enthusiasm of her Western friends with a bit of advice: instead of sending a check to any faraway poor people, they should give a smile to the irritating cases in their own backyard. "Do you know the poor in your town?" she would stubbornly ask when she made stopovers in Germany.

Sometimes she unsettled her coworkers because no subject was too delicate for her to touch on. At the Catholic Congresses in Freiburg and Berlin she insisted on going to visit the inmates of local prisons. She went to Mass with them behind bars, talked to them cheerily about her work, and was embraced by enthusiastic prisoners.

In the leper city of Titagarh a grim-looking individual came in periodically for treatment; Sister Bernard knew him well. "That's Sajada," she said, as she introduced him. "He's a murderer; he did time in prison. He's disfigured, but he has a heart of gold. . . . He does all sorts of illegal things, like brew hard liquor and make bombs. The people hire him out and pay him fairly high prices."

"You brothers and sisters have gotten the best of me," he growled one day. "You love even the bad ones, the ones I get paid to get rid of."

Teresa had, and her companions have, the gift of putting themselves in the place of even their strangest fellow human beings, without immediately drawing up a plan for their complete alteration. They know how much contempt often lurks behind such offers of help. There are lepers in their treatment centers who continue to beg in the streets. Asked why she didn't stop them, Teresa dryly answered, "They find begging interesting."

Surely she must have also thought it strange that "worldlings" should dissipate their energies in a thousand banal activities while never once descending into the depths of their own souls. But she tried slipping into even their skin. "You people in the world may not have the time and the leisure to pray. It's a beautiful gift from God that he lets us have so much time."

A Stir at the Awarding of the Nobel Prize

The unobtrusive nun from Calcutta went briskly along picking up prizes and honors, but not because she was so bent on medals. (The only decoration that she, like all her sisters, wore on her sari was a little cross, fastened with a safety pin on her left shoulder in memory of Christ's suffering for everyone.) No, it was just that she could always use the money for her aid projects, as she would admit with disarming canniness.

And, besides, she made it clear, "Those prizes aren't for me; they're for my people. That's why they have no effect on me, because I know they're not for me. They're for the poor people, who are finally getting noticed.... The world is beginning to find out about them. Just the fact that so much is being written means that people are beginning to feel moved."

She won the international John F. Kennedy Prize for humanitarianism and the John XXIII Peace Prize (for the solemn award ceremonies she went by trolley with the pope's entire diplomatic corps and fifteen cardinals from her settlement house in Rome to the Vatican), the Ceres medal of the World Nutrition Conference, and the Templeton Prize for Progress in Religion.

Of the ten jury members who had to choose the winner of the Templeton Prize, six were Christians, but only one was a Catholic. Prince Philip of England, who delivered the speech at the awarding of the prize on April 25, 1973, conceded that a prize for religion was an absurd idea: "Normally a prize is something for which one needs a competition. But in the case of a prize grounded in religion surely the only persons worthy to receive it are those who didn't compete for it. I can't imagine anyone feeling impelled to do the best religious deed with the goal of winning a prize. And then can any jury, however worthy and unbiased it may be, determine whether one person has been better than another at putting God's work into effect?"

Prince Philip, however, extricated himself from the whole business both elegantly and convincingly by reversing the burden of proof: "In reality it is Mother Teresa who gives this prize its justification.... And so it is Mr. Templeton and the jury who have to be congratulated for Mother Teresa's accepting the prize." What could be learned from her life? "The lesson is

At the awarding of the Nobel Prize in Oslo on December 10, 1979.

simple and ancient: a person's faith gives him the strength for his actions.... Mother Teresa could neither lead this sort of life nor perform such deeds without great faith."

She could have filled a treasure chest with all the medals, honors, and testimonials she was given. They included the Padmashree ("Wonderful Lotus") Prize, the Magsaysay Prize from the Philippines for efforts to spread international understanding, and the Boston Good Samaritan Prize, not to mention two dozen honorary doctorates from, among others, the Universities of Delhi, Pennsylvania, and Cambridge. Just for her the Catholic University of America in Washington, D.C., invented the title "Doctor of Humanity."

A Hindu was asked: "What is Christianity?" He answered: "It is giving." God loved the world so much that he gave up his Son. He gave him to Mary so that she could be his mother. He became a human being like you and me in everything except sin. Jesus too proved his love for us by giving up his life, his own being. He was rich and became poor for you and for me. He gave himself completely up. He died on the cross. But before he died, he made himself into the bread of life, to satisfy our hunger for love. He said: "Unless you eat my flesh and drink my blood, you cannot have eternal life in you." The greatness of his love made him the hungry one, who said: "I was hungry, and you gave me to eat" and "Unless you eat me, you cannot enter into eternal life."

This is Christ's giving. Today too God loves the world. He sends you and me out to prove that he loves the world, that he still has pity for the world. We have to be his love today, his compassion in the world of today. But in order to love, we must have faith; for active faith is love, and active love is service. Jesus made himself into the bread of life, so that we could eat and live and recognize him in the wretched disguise of the poor. In order to be able to love, we must be able to see and feel, and hence Jesus, as we read in the Bible, made the poor into the hope for salvation for you and for me. He said: "What you have done for the least of my brothers, you have done for me."

That's why the work of the Missionaries of Charity is so beautiful. I believe that we actually aren't social workers, but contemplatives in today's world, when we take Jesus literally; for he said: "I was hungry, naked, homeless, and you took care of me." Thus we really touch him twenty-four hours a day, which is why the contemplation and touching of Christ in the poor are so beautiful, so real, so lovable.

Our poor don't need any sympathy or pity, just love and compassion. But we have to know that they are lovable people, great people; this knowledge will lead us to love them and serve them.

Do we really know our poor? They can be in our own family, for love begins at home. Do we know them? Do we know the lonely, the unwanted, the forgotten ones? . . .

This is something that you and I have to understand. St. John says: "How can you say that you love God, whom you do not see, when you do not love your brother, whom you do see?" He uses a very powerful expression when he says: "You are a liar if you say that you love God, but you do not love your brother."

I think we all have to understand that love begins at home. Today we see more and more that all the suffering in the world began at home. Today we don't even have time to look at one another, to talk with one another, to rejoice in one another. We are more and more outside the house, and less and less in contact with one another. . . .

We have to give till it hurts. True love has to hurt. It hurt Jesus to love us. It hurt God to love us, because he had to give. He gave his Son. Today we are here together — I can't give you anything, I have nothing to give — but what I would ask of you is that we all look around and, if we see poor people in our own family, that we begin to love at home until it hurts. Have a smile ready, have time for your fellow men and women! If we know them, then we can tell who our closest neighbor is. Do we know the people around us? There are many lonely people. . . .

In London I went out one day with our sisters and we met a young boy on the streets. I told him: "You shouldn't be here; you should be with your parents." He answered: "Oh, my mother doesn't like me, because I have long hair. Whenever I used to go home, she'd throw me out." We went on. When we came back, we found him there. He had taken an overdose of drugs. We brought him to the hospital. I had to stop and think for a minute: maybe his mother was very busy making collections and doing this and that for the starving people in India. But she had no time, no love — she wasn't concerned; she didn't want her own child. How can we love the poor when we don't love our own children first? Love begins at home....

So let us, as far as possible, pray together, every one of us. What you can do, I can't; and what I can do, you can't. But together we can do something beautiful for God.

Make us worthy, Lord, to serve our fellow human beings all over the world who are living and dying in poverty and hunger. Give them today their daily bread through our hands, give them peace and joy through our understanding love.

— From an address for the awarding of an honorary doctorate
from the University of Cambridge, 1977

Among the highest honors she received was the Nobel Peace Prize in 1979. In a reflective lead article the *Washington Post* said that this event was "meant to remind us of a form of misery that most Europeans and Americans perhaps have never experienced. From time to time Norway's Nobel Prize Committee uses the prize to show the world that there is more than one kind of peace, and that politics isn't the only way to strive for it."

In Oslo the population greeted the little woman in a sari (she had put on over it a knitted wool vest to guard against the December cold of Scandinavia) with a torchlight procession. Mother Teresa cancelled the traditional festive banquet in the Hotel Continental, taking the $7,500 saved, along with the $220,000 award from the prize itself, and around $100,000 from donations collected in Norway back to Calcutta, to help young leper families build homes. "I don't deserve the honor," she insisted. The prize simply meant a recognition of the human dignity of the poor.

And then in the great hall of Oslo University — after inviting the public to pray with her to the one God of all people — she took the West to task. "The greatest destroyer of peace today is the cry of the innocent, unborn child. When a mother can murder her own child in her own womb, what worse crime could there be except for killing one another? ... For me the countries that have legalized abortion are the poorest of all. They are afraid of the little ones; they fear the unborn child."

Mother Teresa begged her listeners not to remain silent any longer, to protect the unborn, to begin with love at home in the family, not to ignore the poor.

"For if you turn your back on the poor, then you are turning it on Jesus. He has made himself hungry, naked, and homeless, so that you and I may have the opportunity to love him!" The poor didn't need sympathy or cold pity. "Our poor are tremendous people. ... They need our respect; they want to be treated with love and attention."

6

"Real Love Has to Hurt"

Where the Roots of Her Strength Lay

Have you already met Jesus?
— Swiss schoolchildren
to Mother Teresa

"We are simple instruments," the modest nun once said, "who do little things and then disappear." She indignantly refused to call her organization of coworkers "The Friends of Mother Teresa." She said she needed help, not veneration. And when a camera-man showed up to do some coverage of her, she sent him on to her coworkers: "Take pictures of *them*; that's who I am."

It was an unusual phenomenon: a woman who was at least as popular as the pope with Christians and non-Christians, who was continuously in the limelight, and who moved with greater ease in front of a TV camera than some rising young stars — this woman had a genuine horror of talking about herself. And this was no feigned modesty, because she had no trouble what-soever politely but pointedly redirecting toward her work all the questions about her own feelings and opinions. No one, not even the most experienced journalists, ever managed to get her to re-veal much of her life story. "The people who write about me," she mused, "know more about me than I do myself." She could be patient in submitting to photographers, because the more or less pious cult of her person brought in money for the children's homes and leprosy centers. But she never tried to look pretty or lovable for the camera; nor would she make a fool of herself for reporters. "I've signed a contract with Jesus," she once remarked sarcastically, "that for every picture they take of me a soul gets freed from Purgatory. These days so many shots have been taken that by now Purgatory is empty."

Long before this she had given up cursing all the ballyhoo and wondering why the media kept focusing on her community as they did: "Others do the same work as I do, perhaps even better. So why do we get this special treatment?"

It was an inimitable Mother Teresa gesture when after a large gathering in a jam-packed German church she was handed a bouquet of flowers: for a long moment she stood there stiffly and awkwardly, the shy little nun of yore. Then she strode quickly to the altar, knelt down, and laid the flowers on the steps, where, according to her firm belief, her friend Jesus dwells among men and women.

"The work is his work and should remain his" — when Mother Teresa said that, it sounded authentic, not dreadfully hollow, like the protests of so many religious leaders who talk about the poor Nazarene while placing suspiciously great emphasis on titles, symbols of power, and tributes. "The work is his work; we are all just his tools that do their little bit and go away."

Father van Exem, an early companion of her community, recalls that one time in a conversation she played dreamily with the stump of a pencil and said: "Look, with me it's something like this. I'm his pencil, so to speak, a little, insignificant stump of a pencil in his hand. He writes with it whatever he wants."

"I Never Think about Money, It Just Comes"

But Teresa's unfeigned simplicity was matched by an organizational talent that many CEOs might have envied. Her sense of where the need in the world was greatest and where she could most meaningfully commit her sisters was legendary. The whole job of administering an unusually effective welfare organization with 4,600 nuns on every continent, with more than 170 schools, homeless shelters, and leper villages in India alone is managed by two sisters with a worn-out old typewriter.

Behind this lies a simple mystery that would be of precious little use to any envious manager: an almost naive trust in God that relieves the sisters of the pressure to be constantly calculating and sets them free for their immediate tasks.

"I never think about money," she would say with a laugh and a shrug of her shoulders. "It just comes. The Lord sends it to us. We do his work; he takes care of the means. If he doesn't give it to us, then that means he doesn't want the work done. Why get excited about it?"

"God will take care of things," she always said. This may have sounded like thoughtless irrationality; but it had, first of all, a solid biblical foundation. As Teresa said: "What a great thing: God promises us that we mean more to him than the flowers and the birds and the grass." And, second, this view was often confirmed by remarkable events, of the sort otherwise known only from the legends of the saints.

One morning in Calcutta the Missionaries had no more rice for the four thousand hungry men and women who came to them every day. The situation was desperate. The people stood there, disappointed, bewildered, some of them enraged. But at around nine o'clock two trucks loaded with bread came roaring up. "It was the largest pile of bread those people had ever seen in their lives," Teresa reported — and then explained the mystery: "The schools had unexpectedly been closed that day, so the bread that would have been used there was sent to the sisters."

"So you see: God is obliging," she added in her artless fashion. "He will never abandon us if we trust him, even if he had to play a trick on people by closing schools."

This didn't prevent Teresa's risky methods of radical trust in

God from occasionally backfiring. Still, when there was absolutely no money left, she would just advise the sisters to beg for what they needed — and life would somehow go on. It would have been much worse, she thought, to depend on earthly safeguards.

She was glad to get contributions, of course; but she didn't think much of long-term agreements: "They mean security," she admitted, "but I want to depend on divine providence." For similar reasons she never accepted government subsidies, because then the modest organizational and bookkeeping arrangements would have had to be hugely expanded and a certain number of sisters, who had been trained at great expense, would have had to wrestle with CPAs and fiscal officers instead of engaging in practical charity.

Teresa perfectly mastered the crazy applied mathematics of this hands-on love: whatever we divide up increases; giving often brings more joy than having; and there are things more precious than material values: "If you have two loaves," a Hindu saying advises, "give one to the poor, sell the other — and buy hyacinths to feed your soul."

Our dependence on God's providence is the solid, living faith that God can and will help us. That he can is obvious, because he is almighty; that he will is certain, because he has promised to in many passages of Holy Scripture, and because he is infinitely faithful in all his promises. Christ encourages us to trust these words: "And whatever you ask in prayer, you will receive if you have faith." And the Apostle Peter bids us cast all our cares on the Lord, who cares for us. And why shouldn't God care for us, since he has sent his Son, and with him everything else? St. Augustine says, "How can you doubt that God will do good for you, since he deigned to take our guilt upon us?"

This has to fill us with trust in divine providence, which maintains even the birds and the flowers. But if God feeds the young ravens, which cry to him, and nourishes the birds that neither sow nor reap, how much more will he care for human beings, whom he has made in his own image and whom he has accepted as his children, if we behave as such, following his commandments and trusting him. I don't want our work to become a business; it should remain a work of love. I would wish you to have complete confidence that God will not disappoint us. Take him at his word, and seek first the kingdom of God; and everything else will be granted to you.

"We Must Fall in Love with God"

Mother Teresa had a relationship with God like a child's with her father. She didn't find him in philosophical models of the world or mystical experiences, but in the flesh-and-blood terms of every person who crossed her path. That was her whole mystery. Her passionate love for the poor, the powerless, the ruined was the response to a love that she had experienced herself and on which she lived. "Love as I have loved you" is inscribed at the foot of the crucifix that one always sees in the chapels of her settlements.

In Delhi Teresa once met an employee of the Indian Ministry of Welfare. He said he was deeply impressed by her work and asked if she would train a group of some twenty colleagues of his — for a fair price, naturally. The officials were to acquire the spirit of the Missionaries, along with their obviously very effective methods.

Fr. Edward Le Joly, the community's spiritual director, reacted rather skeptically when Teresa came to him for advice: "I think you should make it clear to this gentleman," he said, "that the sisters' activity is driven by a special kind of motivation. It's not something that can just be passed along to social workers, unless they share the sisters' faith in Christ." So perhaps two of the social workers might be sent off together every morning to work with the sisters and then in the evening share their impressions with them. But would they really get a taste for the community's program? As he expected, the project never panned out.

In fact the sisters are *not* just social workers with a few good ideas and techniques that anyone could imitate. They exist for Christ, they subsist on Christ; and that distinguishes them from all other "secular" woman teachers or doctors, however selfless. "When we serve the poor, we serve Jesus," Teresa kept repeating. "We care for him, we feed him, we clothe him, we visit and comfort him when we comfort the poor, the abandoned, the orphans, the dying.... Our life has no other meaning and no other motivation."

Whatever you do:
When I was hungry,
you gave me to eat,
when I was thirsty,
you gave me to drink.

Whatever you do for the least
of my brothers, you do for me.
Now enter into my Father's house.

When I was homeless,
you opened your doors to me;
when I was naked,
you gave me your coat;
when I was tired,
you helped me find rest;
when I was frightened,
you took away all my fear;
when I was little,
you taught me to read;

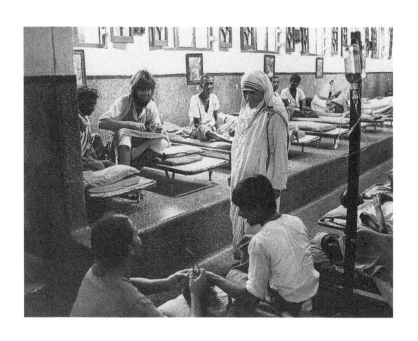

when I was lonely,
you gave me love;

when I was in prison,
you came to my cell;
when I lay on my sickbed,
you nursed me;
in a strange land
you gave me a homeland;
when I was out of a job,
you tried to get me work;

when I was wounded in battle,
you bound up my wounds;
when I longed for kindness,
you held my hand;

when I was a black,
Chinese, or white,
insulted and mocked,
you carried my cross;

when I was old,
you gave me your smile;
when I was restless,
you listened to me patiently;

you saw me covered
with spittle and blood,
you recognized me,
although I was covered
with sweat and filth;

when I was laughed to scorn,
you stood by my side;
when I was happy,
you shared my joy.

The connection between the needy human being and a God kindly disposed to humans — still more, the identification between the God become human in Christ and the human being who has become a wretched nothing — is indissoluble. Teresa thought and felt like St. Irenaeus, the Father of the Church who framed the classical formula of Christian devotion to the world: *Gloria Dei vivens homo*, "The Glory of God is the human person fully alive."

The sisters don't just seek out a calling, based on each one's qualifications and inclinations; they answer a call. "He has chosen us," Teresa always insisted. "We didn't choose him first. But we must respond by making our community into something beautiful for God. . . . We have to fall in love with him." He speaks, he shows the way, he gives the power — that's more important than human ideas and anxieties.

"He would like to live his life in you," Teresa encouraged the people she spoke with. "He would like to see with your eyes, walk with your feet, love with your heart." Nothing else is necessary except to let it be. "He will coax the good out of a person. That's the beautiful thing about God, isn't it? That he can stoop down and let you feel that he depends on you. . . . That's the *most* beautiful thing about God, isn't it? That he's almighty, and yet he doesn't force himself on you."

It surely couldn't be put more simply. One wonders whether Jesus, the artisan's son, who wandered through Galilee with fishermen and farm hands wouldn't have preferred this sort of artless talk to all the rarefied heights of overintellectualized theology.

"I Am Married to Jesus"

"Have you already met Jesus?" a class of Swiss schoolchildren asked "dear Mother Teresa" in a charming letter written in 1979. "We think you have, or he's already talked with you. There's just no other way you could find such strength." Denis and Monika, Martin and Myriam collected money so that the nun could buy food and beds for the poor. But Teresa presumably was even happier that the children had understood so clearly where the roots of her strength lay.

In her iron faith, naturally — as anyone who knew even a little about her life would say. Father van Exem, her old friend and admirer, was asked once what he noticed especially about Mother Teresa, and he answered with a smile: "How small she was in size and how great was her trust in God."

The strength of her devotion, the unconditional resolve with which she gave up her fine profession at St. Mary's High School, simply to be there for the ostracized, the rugged will to live that she showed in the last years of her life as she faced heart attacks, lung problems, kidney pains, and agony from gout in her feet, all in order to work just a few more months or weeks — all that was the expression of an incredibly vital piety that had more to do with steely discipline than with romantic feelings.

But her piety had no trace of the unpitying harshness that often marks religious leaders. Her faith seemed to want to take heaven by storm, restless, single-minded, tearing down all sluggish resistance in her path. She was driven not by duty but by love. When she spoke about her relationship to Christ, it sounded — for all the talk about obedience — not like contractual service, but like a love letter.

Teresa liked to quote the bewitching promises in the prophet Isaiah: "Do not fear, for I have redeemed you; I have called you by name, you are mine.... Can a woman forget her nursing child, or show no compassion for the child of her womb? Even these may forget, yet I will not forget you. See, I have inscribed you on the palms of my hands." And she kept saying over and over again: Men and women are precious, every single one of them; God loves us.

Here is the simple way she justified the vow of chastity, which her sisters, like all religious, take upon themselves: "Jesus gives us for all of life his personal friendship and swathes us in tenderness and love. How wonderful that God himself loves us so tenderly."

Nuns like Teresa have no love-deficit. They don't feel compelled to renounce, but blessed. And they feel themselves thoroughly feminine: "We should not be ashamed to love Jesus with our feelings," as she pointed out.

People often quote her ready reply when an American professor noted skeptically that if she had gotten married, she wouldn't have asked people to deal with one another with a smile. "Oh," she said, "but I am married, and sometimes I find it very hard to smile at Jesus, because he can be very demanding."

A Fragile God

That is why prayer isn't a burdensome duty (at least not as a rule, we may assume), but a need of the heart. And the regular prayer times in all the community's houses (morning Mass, a half-hour meditation, common prayer in the afternoon, and an hour of adoration at night) don't distract them from their "proper work," as secular outsiders suspect. On the contrary, praying opens the heart wide for Christ and for human needs.

"If we pray, we will believe," Teresa explained with the appealingly simple logic that was so typical of her. "If we believe, we will love. If we love, we will serve. Only then can our love for God be transformed into living action through service for Christ, hidden under the wretched cloak of poverty."

But this law also works the other way around. Teresa was once asked how she would get people who had lost their faith back onto the path to heaven. Her answer: "By bringing them into contact with people. Because in people they will find God."

Encounter and silence, contemplation and action always belonged together in her mind. "The more we receive in silent prayer," she said, "the more we can give in our active life. We need silence so that we can touch souls." In other words, "Genuine interior life makes the active life burn brightly and consume everything. It helps us to find Jesus in the dark holes of the shantytowns, to find him in the most heart-rending wretchedness of the poor: the naked God-man on the cross, the sad Man of Sorrows, despised by everyone, crushed by whipping and crucifixion like a worm. . . . *There* is the kingdom of Christ. . . . "

Love as I have loved you — that is the whole mystery. Putting it somewhat mystically, "Being a true Christian means being another Christ for each other." One look at the cross, Teresa used to say, was enough: the head of the dying Christ inclined toward men and women, his arms stretched out as if to embrace them, his open heart — people should approach one another with the same attitude.

The close connection between the Missionaries and the cross allows us to glimpse the deepest spiritual background of their commitment. According to Teresa, they were called "to slake the infinite thirst of a God made man, who has suffered, died, and risen. . . . We are to quench the thirst that Jesus feels for others and for us." That is why in her house chapels under the crucifix stands a second saying that John the Evangelist ascribes to Jesus in his death agony: "I thirst."

Letting oneself be consumed by love like the executed Christ, letting oneself catch his hunger for love — the sisters experience this every morning at the Eucharist, when the bread is broken and the death of Christ is renewed and made present. That is why daily communion is supremely important for Teresa's community, because this becoming one with the Jesus who dies for love represents the strongest motivation for their work. "Try to grasp," she urged her sisters, "how Jesus allows himself to be crushed!"

As Missionaries of Charity we are called to see Jesus' presence above all in the form of bread and to touch him in the disfigured bodies of the poor. When Jesus took the bread, he said: "Take and eat, this is my body, which will be given for you." As he gives himself up, he invites us to grow, thanks to the strength of his love, so that we may do what he has done. Christ's love for us will give us the strength, and urge us on, to give ourselves up for him too. "Let the sisters and the people consume you." We have no right to deny our life to others, through whom we come into contact with Christ....

As for ourselves, we may never separate the Eucharist from the poor and the poor from the Eucharist. You are a real Missionary of Charity if you go to the poor and bring Jesus with you. He appeases my hunger for him, and now I set out to appease his hunger for souls, for love.

That is why Jesus has become bread: to appease our hunger for God. Look at God's humility: He has made himself hungry, so as to appease his divine hunger with our service. Let us pray that none of us may be untrue. Let us pray for our poor, so they too may hunger for God.

The God she believed in was a fragile, vulnerable God: the brother of all suffering, marginalized people. For Mother Teresa Bethlehem and Golgotha belonged close together: in Bethlehem God became a needy child, "God took on a little body, such a little body." And ever since he let this defenseless, abandoned body be nailed to the cross, he has made himself available for us — in a little piece of bread.

Teresa begged her sisters to ask themselves which wounds *they* had inflicted on him with their thoughtlessness and halfheartedness: "Are the nails from me? Is the spittle on his face from me? Which part of his body and his mind has suffered on account of me?" With one careless word one could drive a nail into the heart of another person.

Sharing Wretchedness

When she received the Jawaharlal Nehru Prize, Teresa said that a person will be judged in the sight of God by the measure of love, "depending upon how much we have loved, not how much we have achieved, but how much love there was in what we did." This is a terrible-beautiful truth. In the matchlessly simple formula of a Hindu that Teresa loved to quote, "Christianity is giving."

Teresa was convinced that love, which (in the familiar old truism) is the fruit of an upright faith, needn't be extraordinary, just constant. She once reminded her sisters about the parable of the wise and foolish virgins, noting that, "the oil in our lamps" had to be the little everyday things, "fidelity, punctuality, brief words of kindness, just a simple word for others, the way we are silent, the way we look, speak, and act."

Not just helping because it's needed, but helping with joy; and "joy generally comes from a heart that is burning with love. Don't ever let anything fill you up with so much care that you forget the risen Christ." The point was not just to perform services, but to be attentive: "Considerateness for others is the beginning of holiness. If you learn to be considerate, you will become more and more like Christ, who had a kindly heart and always devoted himself to other people's needs. Your life will be beautiful if you care about others."

The most banal work, seen from this perspective, takes on depth. Work done for love can be inconspicuous, but never sloppy. Work in itself, Teresa was quick to point out, wasn't the calling of the Missionaries: "Our calling is to belong to *him*. That is why I'm ready to do anything: to wash, to sweep, to polish. I am like a mother who has brought a child into the world: all her work — doing the wash, getting up in the middle of the night, and so forth — proves that the little one is hers. She wouldn't do that for any other child, but for her own she's ready to do everything. If I belong to Jesus, I will do everything conceivable for Jesus."

The connection with him is the key. It characterizes the sisters' "method" and makes unmistakably clear the difference between social workers and Missionaries: "Jesus wished to help by sharing our life," Teresa said, "our loneliness, our pains, our death.... We should do the same." Liberation through Christ's sharing our life and through our sharing the lives of our human brothers and sisters. The misery of the poor — not just their material distress, but that of their minds and souls as well — has to be redeemed, "and we must share it, for only if we are one with them, can we redeem them, that is, by bringing God into their lives and bringing them to God."

Sharing misery means more than spending an hour as a volunteer in a hospital or homeless shelter. Sharing misery means going on exhausting long trips, train rides in jammed third-class compartments, bad food (if you're lucky), and often enough excruciating hunger too, sleeping in primitive accommodations, coming down with deficiency diseases. (This was the only point, that Mother Teresa, thank God, wasn't consistent on: she saw to it that her sisters, especially the young ones, always got simple but adequate meals. Emaciated wrecks can't help anyone.) Sharing misery means dirty looks, being "despised and rejected." In extreme cases it means beatings and persecution.

But perhaps it also simply means — holiness. If one listened to Teresa, the wish to become a saint, nowadays generally smiled at, suddenly seemed quite normal; it seemed the obvious prerequisite for a world worth living in, fit for habitation by human

In conversation with Pope John Paul II in Rome on February 5, 1992.

beings. What does holiness mean? Teresa asked almost deprecat-
ingly, and came up with the answer: "Doing God's will with a
smile." In "safer" theological terms, it would mean that Christ
must be able to live his life to the full in us.

In any event holiness, seen that way, is no luxury of a few
particularly gifted (or crazy, if you will) individuals, but "just
a duty for each one of us." It is a highly self-critical claim for
the Missionaries. As Teresa once said: "God told a sister, 'I have
many nuns like you, ordinary good ones. I could pave the streets
with them. But I want sisters who are on fire, I want saints.'...
Wanting to become a saint means stripping myself of everything
that is not God."

Respect instead of Pity

Anyone who wants to fight the misery born of hunger, violence, and fear should presumably make no small demands on himself or herself. A little bit of charity won't do much good for those who have come to grief in society's battle for jobs, money, and living space. As Teresa saw it, the worst sickness wasn't hunger or TB, but the feeling of being unwanted — a sickness for which there is no medicine except authentic devotion based on love.

That is why Teresa tried not to pity people living in filth and misery, but to respect them. Under the crust of wretchedness she discovered their dignity: "You can occasionally skip a meal," she would remind her listeners in the prosperous West, "but what about them? Day after day they suffer hunger. They die all alone. They have no place to stay. Thrown out on the street, they wander around, just trying to survive from day to day. This struggle, this enormous courage is their greatness."

Were those empty words? A horribly injured man from some slum or another once came into her out-patient service. He had been brutally beaten, but he wouldn't give the name of his tormentor — out of fear. When Teresa insisted upon knowing the name of the batterer (and having him charged), the victim ended the conversation with the clinching argument, "His sufferings wouldn't make mine any easier."

The strength of the poor, Teresa said, could teach you a great deal, as could the dignity that they showed in dying: "They radiate joy," she told her surprised audience, "when they return to the source they came from: to the one person who loves them. The people who own a lot of goods and wealth are owned by them. They think the only thing that counts is property and riches. They have a hard time leaving everything behind. The poor have nothing; and so they are free, and this freedom allows them to leave the world behind joyfully."

On one especially bad day she found, as the hours went by, around forty sick and dying people on the streets of Calcutta. Among them was a woman covered with dirty rags, whose life was all but extinguished: "So I just held her hand and tried to comfort her. I have never seen such a beautiful smile on anyone's face. She said only one thing: 'I thank you.' Then she died."

If one wishes to accept Teresa's logic, then the woman made a mistake, because *she* should have thanked the dying person: "She was more anxious to give to me than to take from me. I put myself in her place and wondered what I would have done. I'm sure I would have tried to draw all the attention to myself. I would have said: 'I'm dying. I'm hungry. I'm cold. Call a doctor, a priest, anybody.' But what she did was so beautiful. This woman was more worried about me than I was about her."

Again and again she would tell the story of the four-year-old Hindu boy from Calcutta who had heard that the Missionaries' supply of sugar for the poorest children had run out. "He ran home and told his parents: 'I'll go three days without eating any sugar.' His parents brought him to us, and he brought along with him a little glass full of sugar and said, 'Take this for your children.'"

Or the meeting with the beggar who forced upon her his take for the day, which added up to less than a rupee — a few cents. "I thought for a moment," Teresa said: "If I take the money, then he won't have anything to eat tonight. And if I don't take it, that will hurt his feelings. So I stretched out my hand and took the money. I've never seen so much joy on anyone's face as on the face of that beggar — joy that he too could give something to Mother Teresa." She couldn't buy anything with those few coins, "but when he gave them away and I took them, they became like thousands, because they had been given with so much love."

Poverty Isn't Destiny

Mother Teresa has been blamed for mystifying poverty and for preaching masochism. But she herself distinguished carefully between the freely chosen, deeply symbolic poverty of religious and the misery imposed by force, which flows from unjust social structures. Needless to say, she knew about these larger causes of poverty; and she spoke out loud and clear when the subject arose.

"Poverty is something created by you and me," she said. "It's the result of our refusal to share with others. God didn't create poverty; he only created us. The problem will not be solved until we become capable of giving up our greed." At the hour of our death, she prophesied, the poor will be our judges. Christ will pass sentence on us, depending upon whether we have recognized him in them and acted accordingly.

Once again, her relations with the poor can't be understood solely from the standpoint of common sense, but only as the consistent conclusion of the Gospels, where Christ equates himself with the least of his brothers and sisters: "If you turn your back on them, Christ turns his back on you." What was human misery but Christ's "wretched disguise"?

Mother Teresa wanted to show the have-nots, the marginalized and despised, what she believed in, with every fiber of her passionate heart: God has an infinite love for every single person. Of course, no poor person will believe such a thing just on the strength of sermons. And that's why Teresa also never left any doubt that love is a harsh business. "We have to give until it hurts," she used to say. "Real love has to hurt!" Because loving humans hurt God too: He gave his Son up to death.

One time a group of business people came to present her with the proceeds raised at a banquet. Mother Teresa looked at them a little skeptically, then she observed with some hesitation: "I hope you're not just giving from your superfluity. You have to give something that costs you something. It should be a sacrifice for you; you have to give up something that you've become attached to. Then your gift will have a value before God as well. Then you will really become the brother of the poor people who lack the most basic necessities."

Putting it more drastically, she once said: "Don't we sometimes treat the poor like a garbage can into which we throw everything we can't eat or don't need? 'I can't eat that, so the poor get it. I can't use this garment, so I can give it to the poor.' Am I sharing poverty with the poor if I act that way?" Well-fed persons with an inclination to charity, she said, could find the proper standards for this sort of love, a love that costs, by turning to those who are themselves suffering bitter need. Mother Teresa never got tired of talking about their greatness.

In Melbourne I visited an old man, who nobody knew existed. I saw that his room was in wretched shape, and I wanted to clean it up. He stopped me: "I'm doing fine." I didn't say anything, and finally he let me do it.

In his room there was a wonderfully beautiful lamp, all covered with dust. I asked him: "Why don't you turn this lamp on?" "For whom? Nobody ever visits me." Then I asked him: "Will you light the lamp if the sisters come to visit you?" "Yes, if I hear a human voice, I'll turn it on."

Recently he sent word to me: "Tell my friend that the lamp she turned on in my life is still burning."

These are the people whom we have to get to know. If we do get to know them, we'll learn to love them, and this love will teach us to serve them. Let's not be satisfied with just giving them money. Money isn't enough. You can always earn money. But they need your hands, so that you can serve them. They need your hearts, so that you can love them.

                                                    —From the address given at the awarding of the Templeton Prize

7

"We Were Made to Bring Joy into the World"

Forty-Six Hundred "Teresas"
Live with the Poorest of the Poor

What a delightful idea.
—Malcolm Muggeridge on Teresa's offer
to work as a flight attendant

Al Hudaydah, Yemen, in the 1960s. The Missionaries of Charity got it into their heads to free the lepers all crowded together in a remote village and help them to a life befitting a human being. "Have you ever seen the movie *Ben Hur?*" one of the sisters would later ask. "That's about the way you have to imagine the situation there.... We had a lot of trouble just gaining access to the village. The way was blocked with junk and garbage. We had to wade through knee-deep filth. There were no houses there at all; the people lived in a kind of caves dug into the hills. When they saw us come, they ran away and hid themselves in the caves. The children ran for their lives."

It took the sisters weeks to overcome the mistrust of the lepers, who until then had known nothing but hatred and persecution. Then they built houses, laid out gardens, and taught their new friends trades. Soon there were 120 lepers living in a well-furnished home in Al Hudaydah; as many as 600 a day — including some from communist South Yemen — came for out-patient care; and around 100 girls were trained in handicrafts.

Melbourne, Australia, April 1970. Teresa goes with five sisters in search of a house. They find one that has long been empty and is accordingly dilapidated. That same day the six of them sweep the trash out of the building, seal the roof, and set up one of the front rooms for sleeping. Since there isn't enough space, one of them has to spend the night under a table. But the new settlement is on its feet.

That is the spontaneous, consistent, and purposeful way things usually go once the Missionaries discover yet another focal point of destitution. Their headquarters are still located in Calcutta, on Lower Circular Road. Here the sisters' operations are planned out: the establishment of new houses, immediate measures to fight famine, and vocational programs for young people in the slums.

Starving youths whom Mother Teresa used to collect at Calcutta's central train station have learned to make small items of furniture and sell them in the market. In all this one sees not a trace of bureaucracy, crisis management committees, or the usual time-consuming office routines. There are no huge jumbles of waste paper, no interminable conferences. All sorts of personal contacts see to it that the projects don't grind to a halt, but develop efficiently — with the power of persuasion that grows only out of person-to-person contact.

Three Saris and a Straw Mattress

In 1950, just two years after its beginning in Calcutta, Pope Pius XII confirmed Teresa's new congregation — an unusually quick approval by Roman standards. Every week new candidates kept coming in to Mother Teresa. The vocation crisis of the

Mother Teresa and the orphaned children.

1960s swept past this old-fashioned community and its Spartan lifestyle without leaving a trace.

"Very, very few have left us," *Mataji* once calculated, not without pride. "You could count them on the fingers of your hand." On the other hand, contempt for those who have bailed out was never Teresa's way. "We are all human," she said and added one more obligation to the rules: "Pray for all those who once belonged to our order. May God protect and keep them in his love."

No doubt the great majority of them knew what they were getting into: an incredibly hard life under extreme conditions. The Missionaries of Charity want to be there for the lost, those for whom the word "poor" seems much too kind: "Not the poor," Teresa said, "but the poorest of the poor" were her community, "the people who don't go to church, because with the rags they have on they don't dare to. The poor are the ones who don't eat because they no longer have the strength to; those who collapse on the street and know that they are dying while the living pass them by without so much as casting a glance at them. They are the ones who don't cry because they have no more tears left."

Those who wish to share the misery of these marginal lives can't be overly demanding. The sisters live in threes and fours in little rooms that they keep changing so as not to accumulate any idle comforts (Teresa herself made do with a cell which had only a bed and a wooden table, on which she wrote out her correspondence while the others slept). They eat, on enamelware plates, a very simple diet with a lot of rice and vegetables. They have no TV sets in their houses, at most a radio to keep up on the news; and even when it's 113 degrees and in the murderous humidity they do without electric fans, which in India are status symbols of the well-off.

Teresa never budged an inch from the conviction that her community was there for the poor, and the only guarantee of that was a radically poor way of life. Other orders too had, at first, helped the poor. What became of them? "Gradually they came to serve both rich and poor. And finally just the rich." She wanted to block such a development from the outset.

Every sister has three sets of clothing — each consisting of a cotton habit and a blue-fringed sari: she wears one while the second is in the wash and the third is drying. Apart from that her only belongings are a pair of sandals, a wash basin, a crucifix, and a straw mattress. That's all. But this doesn't frighten off those who have grasped what the Missionaries of Charities are after.

Before God our poverty is a humble recognition and acceptance of our human frailty, our incapacity, and our nothingness. It is the knowledge of our neediness, which finds expression in the hope of him, in the readiness to receive everything from him, the Father. Our poverty should be truly evangelical — lovable, cheerful, cordial, always ready for a sign of love. Poverty is love, and only then is it renunciation. To love one must give. To give one must be free from egoism. In the longing to share the poverty of Christ and that of our poor:

- *we are ready to have everything in common and to share everything with the sisters of the congregation;*

- *we accept from relatives, friends, or benefactors nothing whatsoever for our personal use. Everything given to us we return to our superiors for use in the community or in the service of the poor;*

- *we eat the food of the people in whose country we live, and we prefer whatever is cheaper. The food should be healthy and abundant enough so that we can stay in good health, which is essential, given the work that our calling demands;*

- *our houses should be simple and modest, places where the poor can feel at home;*

- *we travel, whenever we have an opportunity, on foot; or else we use the simple, readily available means of public transportation;*

- *we sleep in common dormitories without private space, like the poor;*

- *in our material and intellectual needs we and our poor are completely dependent on divine providence. . . .*

On the cross our Lord possessed nothing. The cross was given to him by Pontius Pilate, the nails and crown of thorns by the soldiers. He was naked, and when he died, the cross, the nails, and the crown were taken away. He was wrapped in a linen cloth given him by a kindhearted person and buried in a grave that wasn't his. . . .

Poverty is necessary, because we serve the poor. If they complain about their food, we can say: We eat that too. If they say, It was so hot last night I couldn't sleep, we can answer: We were hot too. The poor wash their own clothes, they go barefoot: so do we. We have to humble ourselves to exalt them. The heart of the poor opens when we can assure them that we live the way do. Sometimes they have only a bucket of water. So do we. They have to stand in line; so do we. Food, clothing, everything, should be the way the poor have it. We fast. Our fasting consists in eating what we get without choosing.

Although Christ was rich, he emptied himself. Here lies the contradiction. If I wish to be poor like Christ — who despite his wealth became poor — I have to do the same thing. Nowadays there are people who want to be poor and to live with the poor, but they would like to be free to dispose of things as they wish. Having such freedom means being rich. They want both, which they can't have. That is another kind of contradiction.

Our poverty is our freedom. Our poverty consists in renouncing our freedom to dispose of things, to choose and possess them. The moment I use things and dispose of them as if they belonged to me is the moment I stop being poor.

We have to strive for the true spirit of poverty. It manifests itself in the love with which we live the virtue of poverty as the imitation of Christ, who chose it as the companion of his earthly life among us. Christ wasn't bound to live a life of poverty, but by choosing it he taught us how important poverty is for our sanctification.

The community was still fairly young when a certain Sister Andrea won a gold medal in a medical school examination. She happily came home and showed Mother Teresa her award. Teresa congratulated her, but then she dryly asked: "Now, sister, what do you want to do with it?" Sister Andrea said she hadn't thought about that yet, whereupon *Mataji* replied: "But you have to think about it! You don't need the medal. It doesn't mean anything. You're not opening a practice. You're not writing M.D. after your name. You want to work among the poor. What good will a gold medal do there?"

Sister Andrea found that fairly logical. She brought the pretty medal back; a young colleague, who had finished second, got it instead — and both of them beamed: the young man because he now had a trophy to hang in his room and Sister Andrea because she felt splendidly free.

Poverty, freely chosen poverty, leads to independence. Francis of Assisi discovered that long ago: "If we had possessions," he said, "we would also need weapons to defend ourselves." It also leads to bravery, because what does a poor person have to lose?

After a few years Sister Andrea took over the leadership of Teresa's settlement in the Bronx. She found a man on the sidewalk whose legs were covered with running sores. As a doctor she knew that he urgently needed treatment in a hospital. She called for an ambulance, but a patrol car responded instead: ambulances had long been avoiding that notorious neighborhood.

One of the policemen immediately started shouting at the man, as he no doubt was used to doing with bums and alcoholics. In sheer terror — perhaps he also had something to hide — the sick man ran into an entryway and disappeared. Now Mother Superior Andrea summoned all her courage and told the policeman calmly but decisively: "Sir, this man was Jesus for me; and what you just said to him you said to Jesus." The cop's jaw dropped; he had never heard anything like that before. Finally he apologized to the resolute sister, meek as a whipped dog, and began to look for the frightened-off patient in all the alleys and backyards for more than an hour. Never again, he promised the nun, would he treat anyone like that.

Better to Be Friendly Than to Work Miracles

What visitors find most amazing is the joy radiated by these sisters who are slaving away under indescribably harsh conditions. This is not the put-on, slightly infantile gaiety typical of some Christian communities. The Missionaries live what their foundress expressed this way: "True holiness consists in doing God's will with a smile." For what is joy but the spontaneous consequence of love? It makes the sisters happy that they can help. Their laughter isn't a part of their job; it's genuine.

"The goodness has to show on your face," Teresa charged them, "in your eyes, in your smile, in the heartiness of your greeting. You always have to give a joyful smile to the children, the poor, the suffering, the lonely. You shouldn't just take care of them; you must also give them your heart." When the convent in Melbourne was consecrated in 1973, she gave her sisters a piece of advice as sober as it was wise: "I don't want to hear that you're working miracles, but unfriendly when you go about it. I'd rather have you make mistakes, but be friendly."

Candidates have to wait three years before taking their vows (which in the case of the Missionaries include a special promise to serve only the poorest of the poor). Their preparation is made up of spiritual training, practical instruction in, for example, nursing, social work, medicine, or law, and, if necessary, general education. Those who don't already speak English take a language course, since English is the international language of the community.

The new member of the order can do her novitiate in Calcutta, Rome, Manila, Nairobi, San Francisco, or Warsaw, in very sparely furnished settlements. The first one in Rome was located in the poor neighborhood of Acquedotto Felice, which takes its name from the ruins of an ancient aqueduct and which is exactly like the huts and crooked little houses all around it.

Temporary vows are made after two years and renewed every

year. Not until eight years after entering the order does a nun take her permanent vows. Before that she is sent home to her family for three weeks to go through one more round of serious reflection on her decision.

Families can be a sticking point. In entering the order a young woman generally faces a much harder break with parents and siblings than if she were getting married or entering a profession. Teresa was sensitive to this and tried to ease such burdens.

Josepha Gosselke, long-time spokeswoman for the association of the Missionaries' German coworkers, tells of an indignant father who broke with his daughter after she defied him by going to Mother Teresa in Calcutta. On her next trip to Germany Teresa insisted on meeting this bitterly disappointed man. She moved up the date for the vows ceremony so that it could take place in Freiburg with the whole family and many friends in attendance. It was a lovely service, and afterward the father gave a moving speech with tears in his eyes. On another occasion Mother Teresa went to Wattenscheid in North Rhine-Westphalia to visit the grave of the parents of a sister with whom she had become very close. She left at the cemetery the flowers she had just received for her own birthday.

From Manila to the Bronx

Today 4,600 sisters in 107 countries are trying to live like Mother Teresa. They have built well over 500 clinics, orphanages, schools, leprosy centers, and homes for dying (once in print most of the figures prove too low). Since 1965, when a settlement was founded in Caracas, Venezuela, the sisters have expanded overseas, to Australia, New Guinea, Ethiopia, Yemen, Peru, Mexico, Guatemala, Jordan. As Mother Teresa said, "There is no place in the world free from poverty and injustice."

Her greatest wish was always to go as quickly as possible to wherever she and her sisters were needed. She received a free railway pass from the Indian government, and, in order to get the same preferential treatment for air travel, she offered one airline, in all seriousness, to work off her fare by serving as a flight attendant. This struck Malcolm Muggeridge as a "delightful idea," and he was saddened when her suggestion was turned down.

"We were created to bring joy into the world," she said, "so that we could love one another and love God." And so it was good not to tie oneself down to any one spot, but to hurry back and forth across the earth; for such haste is a proof of how ardent one's love is.

The forty-six hundred sisters — so many lovable Teresas — never establish themselves permanently. In the Third World they live in primitive huts or simple mud houses, blending in with the rest of the slums. In the developed countries they choose rented apartments and unobtrusive row houses. When some well-meaning friends in Venezuela put up a nice little house with a refrigerator, bath, and handsome furniture, the sisters unhesitatingly turned the building into a home for the dying and moved into huts they had built themselves.

In Manila, which, like the rest of the Philippines, has no free medical care, the Missionaries set up an out-patient center. There they cook meals of meat, fresh fish, vegetables, and fruit for the undernourished children susceptible to TB. In the vicinity of Port-au-Prince, Haiti, they run several pharmaceutical dispensaries and schools for the young people of the slums.

In Rotterdam they have rented a dilapidated house in the middle of the city, where they lend a hand to mentally handicapped old people and shelter children of mixed races who have been turned out because of their dark skin. In New York they have settled into an abandoned convent in the South Bronx, where they care for old and sick people who no longer dare to go out into streets ruled by youth gangs and drug lords. In a day-care center they try to protect children from the omnipresent violence. They have accommodated mentally disturbed women in a home; and on the weekends they visit prisoners on Rikers Island who have been written off by their families. In Los Angeles the Missionary Brothers of Charity work among street gangs.

The brothers now can be found in most countries as a counterpart to the sisters. They wear no special uniform and have become active mostly in places where naked violence prevails. They take care of alcoholics and mental patients, drug addicts and young criminals. As their rule declares, they are supposed to be "like the first Christians" as "messengers of the Word of God to the poorest in spirit."

Europe Has Ghettoes Too

Mother Teresa wanted to be on the spot whenever and wherever there was a cry for help. Sometimes such cries had an illustrious source: in 1968 a private letter from Pope Paul VI arrived in Calcutta with two plane tickets, a check for over $10,000, and comments about the wretched living conditions in the suburbs of Rome. A few weeks later Mother Teresa and Sister Frederick flew to Rome, took a look around in the slums, signed up a few construction workers, grabbed bricklayers' trowels themselves, and began to set up an out-patient center and a kindergarten. (The latter was especially important, because the mothers have to earn extra money. Most of the families have come to Rome from southern Italy in hopes of well-paid work, but with the jobs that the men get they often can afford only primitive shacks.)

The "Indian sisters," as the Romans affectionately call them, visit the shabby homes of the sick and poor; they bring hot milk and sandwiches to the homeless in the parks and subway stations where they bed down for the night. For the elderly who have no regular place to stay they have established a shelter near the train station where they can wash and get a warm meal. As a sideline, so to speak, the sisters give religious instruction to the little children, whose families are often fairly alienated from the church. No one seems to mind: everyone here loves the "Indian sisters," and in the markets people give them vegetables and chickens for their protégés.

The situation is completely different in London, where one can likewise find bitter material distress, but also many prosperous people who live completely isolated in their comfortable apartments. These are men and women whose death no one notices, until days or even weeks later an unpleasant odor alarms their hitherto uninterested neighbors. "In England," Teresa realized, "people are suffering from loneliness. There's no lack of bread, but of human attention. For us that's the hungry Christ." So the sisters have not only organized soup kitchens and outings for the homeless in Kilburn (London) and Liverpool; they not only supply heaters and furniture to old people in run-down apartments. They also take the trouble to find the lonely, the people no one looks after. They visit and do chores for them, to bring them back to life. One British volunteer named Mary reports how happy her clients are when, after the food has been distributed, she sits down beside them, looks at their picture albums from better days, and asks about their problems.

In 1971 in Northern Ireland, at the high point of the unrest, which was something like a civil war, Mother Teresa suddenly arrived in Belfast to set up a base of operations in the poor Catholic neighborhood of Ballymurphy. This was a cheerless ghetto with a population of Catholic underdogs who felt threatened by the Protestant majority and abandoned by the British crown. The unemployment rate at that time was 47 percent. British soldiers patrolled the streets, always on the lookout for snipers. Teresa the arch-Catholic simply went to the meetings of Quakers and Presbyterians and spoke of her own experiences with injustice and marginalization. That seemed more important to her than material help.

Eight years later the first settlement in Germany was established. In a satellite town of Essen, a social hot spot with many endangered young people, the sisters rented a few rooms in a multistory house with seventy senior citizens' apartments, where they set up their miniature convent. The five young missionaries from Germany, Italy, India, and Poland moved into a row house on the edge of the city, where they take in stranded and homeless people for a maximum of three months, along with alcoholics, drug addicts, and abused women. Although there is a strict ban on alcohol in the house and they have to help out with cleaning up, peeling potatoes, etc., the residents are fiercely loyal to the sisters. Sister Thomas More from India is asked whether she is ever afraid of the toughs out on the street. "Oh no," she says with a ringing laugh, "they all respect us completely. If one of them was to get out of line, all the rest would gather round to protect us." Contacts with the parish are working extremely well. One group of women goes off regularly to bakeries in search of day-old cakes and cookies, which then become dessert for the homeless. The operation is supported entirely by donations; there are no subsidies from the city or the church.

At the central train station in Munich or the Marienplatz in the heart of the city the sisters in their exotic-looking outfits have been engaged for some years now in their unconventional work on behalf of the homeless and runaways. In an erstwhile cash-only liquor store they have set up their little convent; from there they head out into the streets and squares of the inner city, visiting the mentally disturbed and alcoholics. At the evening hour of adoration passersby are always welcome.

The Missionaries have settled in Hamburg, Mannheim, Chemnitz, Zurich, and Vienna. "Some fifty forgotten families and seniors who are barely eking out a living somewhere in the canyons of the capital are on the visiting list of the Teresa Sisters," writes journalist Toni Görtz from Berlin-Kreuzberg. The sisters drag coal buckets to people's apartments, where they have time for longish conversations — or simply get a broken grandfather clock started up again. Their St. Joseph's Soup Kitchen is also much in demand. It's true, Sister Lumina says, that nobody in Germany has to go hungry; everything is financially regulated. "But many people come to us, because they sense that they're welcome."

Love Begins at Home

In Berlin and Munich, in London, Rotterdam, and New York the Missionaries of Charity see another face of poverty. It has nothing to do with undernourishment and wretched living conditions, but a lot to do with a lack of humanity and human attention. As Teresa used to say, hunger can also be created by not enough love and recognition, homelessness by hatred of strangers and the refusal to talk with them.

In the rich countries she saw countless young people in "invisible homes for the dying." These were the ones whose parents met their children's material needs without taking any interest in their lives. By the same token, many old people were awaiting death in total isolation. Teresa told of an old, extremely rich married couple: the husband was half-blind, the wife deranged. In desperation he begged her to send one of her sisters to the house: "Our children are all gone, and we are dying of loneliness. We yearn for the precious sound of a human voice."

For this reason when she made appearances in the West Teresa wasn't too happy with the public's endless questions about poverty in Calcutta and Bombay, Beirut and Dar es Salaam. She liked to turn the tables on her audience and say: "What I would ask of you is to take a look around; and when we see the poor in our own families, let's begin to love at home, until it hurts."

Some people, she said, were busy organizing collections for the hungry in India, while not having any time or love left over for their own children.

Even today Jesus isn't recognized by his own, when he comes into his world. He comes in the emaciated bodies of our poor; as a matter of fact he also comes in the rich, who are practically stifled by their wealth. He comes in the loneliness of their hearts, and when there is no one there to love them. Jesus comes to you and to me; and often, very often, we go right past him....

Today Christ appears to us in the men and women who are unwanted, unemployed, shoved aside, hungry, naked, and homeless. To the state and to society they seem useless, and nobody has time for them. As Christians who want to be worthy of the love of Christ, if our love is true, you and I have to go find them and help them. They are there so that we may find them.

Everywhere we find lonely people, who are often known only by their room number. Where are we? Do we even know that such people exist? Perhaps right next door to us there is a blind man who would be happy to have us read him the newspaper. Perhaps there is a rich man who has no one to visit him. He may have a lot of possessions, he may be almost choking on them; but he has nobody to touch him, and he needs your touch....

Don't look for God in faraway lands — he isn't there. He is right nearby. Just keep the light burning, and you will always see him. Watch and pray. Keep turning the lamp on, and you will see his love and recognize how good the God is whom you love.

Lord, open our eyes,
so that we may recognize
our brothers and sisters.

Lord, open our ears,
so that we may hear
the cry of the hungry,
the cold, the fearful,
and the oppressed.

O Lord, open our hearts,
so that we may love one another,
as you love us.

Renew in us your spirit,
Lord, make us free and united.

Teresa's community was also one of the first in the Catholic Church to face the challenge posed by the victims of AIDS. They jumped in and lent a hand, without using the opportunity to preach, as often happened early on. In New York the sisters regularly visited HIV patients who had been transferred from Sing Sing Prison to St. Clare's Hospital or Mount Sinai.

In 1985, with help from Cardinal John O'Connor, the Missionaries opened their first house for AIDS patients. It's hard, Sister Dolores says, to handle the irrevocable last stage of life. "So we took the time to create a family atmosphere among them. We all ate together; we talked, prayed, and played together." Some of them managed to revive the shattered relationship with their families. "And as we grew in number, the patients began looking after one another; it was a wonderful experience."

The Missionaries have AIDS houses in Washington, Baltimore, Atlanta, and San Francisco, in Guwahati (in the Indian state of Assam) — right next to the "Golden Triangle," the biggest emporium in Asia for heroin and opium — in Bombay, Brazil, Honduras, Spain, and Portugal. They are also working with AIDS patients in Haiti and Africa, where the situation is especially bad.

Teresa never asked people how they had caught the virus. "We just see their need and take care of them," she said. "I believe that with AIDS God is saying something to us, that he's giving us a chance to show our love." The most terrible thing for her was always the thought that any person had to feel unwanted and rejected. Was AIDS a divine punishment? "No one," she insisted, "should deliver such a judgment. It's God's mystery."

Caring for AIDS patients is something like nonstop crisis intervention. But Teresa's sisters and brothers also respond to acute emergencies, such as the catastrophic flooding around Calcutta, which left twelve hundred families homeless, or a devastating earthquake in Guatemala. When something like that happens, they are always on the spot, bringing food, building shelters, helping to rescue people buried in landslides.

In 1991, when the Gulf War broke out, Teresa couldn't help. But her heart bled, and she wrote a letter to Presidents George Bush and Saddam Hussein, begging them to reach a reconciliation. In the short run there might be winners and losers in this butchery. "But what price will the people have to pay who are broken, disabled, and lost?" No one answered her letter, but after much of Baghdad had been destroyed by U.S. bombers, Teresa founded a home there for crippled and undernourished children.

To President Bush and Saddam Hussein

54A, A.J.C. Bose Road
Calcutta 16
January 2, 1991

Dear President George Bush
and President Saddam Hussein,

I come to you with tears in my eyes and God's love in my heart, to beg for the poor and for those who will be poor if the war that we all fear should come. I beg you with all my heart to strive for God's peace, to work hard at it and to find the way to reconciliation.

Both of you wish to represent your point of view and to take care of your people, but first listen to the one who came into the world to teach us peace. You have the might and the power to destroy God's presence and likeness. His men, his women, and his children. Please obey the will of God. God has created us to be loved by his love, not destroyed by our hatred.

In the short run, this war that we all fear may, perhaps, have winners and losers, but that never can or will justify the loss of so many lives that your weapons will cause.

I come to you in the name of God, whom we all love and share, to beg for the innocent and poor in the world and for those who will be made poor by the war. They will suffer the most, for they have no possibility of fleeing. I beg you on my knees for these people. They will suffer; and then we will be to blame, because we have not done everything in our power to protect them and to love them. I implore you for the orphans and the widowed, who will remain behind alone, because their parents, husbands, brothers, and children have been killed. I implore you to save these people.

I plead for those who will be disabled and mutilated. They are God's children. I plead for those who will have no more shelter, no food, and no love. Please look upon these people as though they were your children. Finally I plead to you for those who will lose the most precious thing that God has given us, life. I implore you to spare our brothers and sisters. Yours and ours, for they have been given to us by God, so that we may love and respect them. We have no right to destroy what God has given us. Please, please make God's will and understanding your own. You have the power to bring war into the world or to make peace. PLEASE CHOOSE THE PATH OF PEACE.

I, my sisters, and our poor pray so much for you. The whole world is praying that you may open your hearts to God in love. You may win the war, but what price will the people have to pay who are broken, disabled, and lost?

I appeal to you — to your love, your love for God and your fellow men and women. In the name of God and in the name of those whom you will make poor: don't destroy life and peace! Let love and peace triumph, so that your name may be remembered for the good that you have done, the joy that you have brought, and the love that you have shared.

Please pray for me and my sisters, who are trying to love the poor and to serve them, because they belong to God and are loved by him. And too we pray with our poor for you. We pray that you will love and care for what God has so lovingly entrusted to your custody.

May God bless you, now and for ever.

God bless you!

M. TERESA, M.C.

— Letter at the beginning of the Gulf War

"I'm a Revolutionary Too"

It remains a mystery how, amid these hundreds of houses that she had conjured up out of the ground with her tireless imagination, she was able to maintain an overview. On Vatican territory she set up a home for the Eternal City's homeless. In Moscow she personally asked for permission to construct a house near

A meeting in Jerusalem with PLO chief Yasir Arafat, who gave her a check for her work.

Chernobyl for the victims of radiation sickness after the reactor melt-down.

In Jordan the Missionaries care for the poor, for physically and mentally handicapped persons, for abandoned children, both Muslim and Christian. The Muslims call them *hajjis*, because they wear white robes like pilgrims to Mecca. In the Gaza Strip they try, as they shuttle back and forth between Jews and Arabs, to alleviate the sufferings of refugees. In Latin America the sisters are strongly committed to pastoral care: "We do there practically everything that under normal circumstances the parish priest does among us," one of them reports, "except for hearing confessions and saying Mass."

In 1979 Mother Teresa founded her first settlement in a communist country. In 1991 she got authorization from her homeland of Albania; and in four months she built five houses there for poor people, while simultaneously hammering out plans for Rumania, Cambodia, Cuba, and China. There is poverty — especially spiritual poverty — in the socialist world too, as she matter-of-factly observed.

In Ethiopia a very self-assured governor wondered out loud about her request to build a hospital. "Don't you know," he gruffly asked her, "that we have a revolution here that takes care of such things?" Unflapped, she countered: "I'm a revolutionary too; but my revolution consists only in love."

To be sure, she had failures as well. She sent some nuns to the mountainous Indian region of Simla, where it gets ice-cold in the winter. But the sisters came from the hot and humid lowlands, and they couldn't bear the climate. Besides, in those sparsely populated areas there was so little to do that they finally gave up in complete exhaustion. In Sri Lanka, where foreign missionaries hadn't received entry visas for more than ten years, Teresa's forces were at first given a surprisingly warm reception; but then they too were ejected from the country. There were similarly dismal experiences in Vietnam and Northern Ireland. And, of course, every now and then a pair of rowdies in Berlin-Kreuzberg will scream at the young women in white and blue saris, "Go back to India!"

"The future is not in our hands," Mother Teresa used to say in such situations. "We can only act today." But she would soon be defiantly asserting, "If there are poor people on the moon, then let's go there too!"

Finally, she not only had to keep her nuns busy — the several thousand members of her order who were bursting with energy. She also had at least eighty thousand coworkers on her hands: circles of friends who organized neighborhood auxiliaries to visit lonely men and women in nursing homes, to sew baby clothes for Indian babies and collect money for Teresa's other activities. In 1993 Mother Teresa dissolved the coworkers organization — out of sheer anxiety that with all its boards of directors, connections, and bank accounts, it might turn into a monstrously bloated bureaucracy that would pervert the order's original meaning into its opposite. It was a typical decision for Teresa the creative maverick.

In a series of highly personal circular letters she asked her lay friends to try something different, something that might be more difficult: to help the Missionaries in the future not through an organization, but through direct aid to the settlements, or by taking care of the poverty and distress in their own neighborhoods. "Each and every one of you," she wrote, "can pray, and make his or her home into another Nazareth without the Coworkers Association. . . . Be the sunshine of God's love in your own family, your neighborhood, and your city!"

She happily told about the young men and women — Catholics, Protestants, non-Christians — who came from all over the world to Calcutta to serve the poor there for a given period of time and to share in the community's worship. "And when they go back home, none of them is the same person." Even older people were among the helpers: "Recently a seventy-seven-year-old man, blind in both eyes, came to Calcutta and wanted to help out for a few days. He went to the home for the dying and gave massages to some patients there. He also helped wash them. Afterward I spoke with him. He kept saying, 'Bearers of God's love!' And he smiled."

We will make this year a year of peace, in a special way. In order to be able to do that, we shall try to speak more to God and with God, and less to and with human beings. Let us preach the peace of Christ, as he did. He went about doing good. He didn't give up his works of love just because the Pharisees and others hated him or tried to ruin his Father's work. He simply went around doing good.

Cardinal Newman has written: "Let me spread your fragrance everywhere I go; let me preach without preaching, not with words, but through example, through contagious strength, through the invis-

ible influence of what I do, through the visible fullness of the love that my heart cherishes for you." Our works of love are nothing but works of peace. Let us do them with greater love and greater effectiveness, each and every one of us in his or her daily work, in our home, with our neighbor. It is always the same Christ who says:

> *I was hungry — not for food, but for the peace that comes from a pure heart.*

> *I was thirsty — not for water, but for the peace that extinguishes the passionate thirst for the passion of war.*

> *I was naked — not stripped of clothing, but of the beautiful dignity of men and women.*

> *I was homeless — not without a roof made of bricks, but without a heart that understands, protects, and loves.*

This year let us be those things for Christ in our neighbor, wherever the Missionaries of Charity and their coworkers are. Let us radiate the peace of God, and thus kindle his light and quench all hatred and love of power in the world and in the hearts of all men and women. Let the Missionaries of Charity and their coworkers in every country where they are smile and meet God in everybody, everywhere they go.

—From a letter to the coworkers

There are also volunteer helpers who commit themselves to work for months or years in the houses of the Missionaries and without whom the order would never have been able to cover so much ground. In Calcutta a group of women and men has been formed that every day cares for as many as forty youngsters at the Howrah train station. The "kids" there live like wild animals in the jungle of the big city. Babies are born on the platforms, the bigger boys rape the little girls and boys — while the Calcutta police have long since given up worrying about such commonplace problems. Instead they have several times arrested Mother Teresa's coworkers for disturbing the peace.

Still the volunteers persevere in trying to get the children away from the train station. Meantime they have managed to get hold of a doctor, a nurse, and a few teachers. The teachers instruct in a very relaxed, playful style, using Hindi, Bengali, and English; and they actually succeed again and again in placing a few of the train station children in regular schools.

Mother Teresa used to call "our treasure" a final group of helpers that she prized: the sick. They "adopt" a sister or a brother and offer up their pain for them. And the brother or sister offers up his or her work for the sick person. Teresa once confessed to having an "alter ego," a woman in Belgium: "Every time that I have something especially hard to do, she's the one who stands behind me and gives me strength and courage."

Dear Lord, may I see you today and every day in the person of your sick and, as I nurse them, may I serve you.

Even when you present yourself in the unhandsome disguise of the irritable, the demanding, or the unreasonable, may I recognize you and say: "Jesus, my patient one, how sweet it is to serve you."

Lord, give me this seeing faith; then my work will never get tedious. I will always find joy in bearing the moods and fulfilling the wishes of all poor sufferers.

O dear sick people, how doubly dear you are to me, when you embody Christ; and what an advantage it is for me to be allowed to care for you.

Lord, make me receptive to the dignity of my high calling and to its many responsibilities. Don't allow me to dishonor them by slipping into coldness, unfriendliness, and impatience.

And, O God, since you, Jesus, are my patient one, deign to be a patient Jesus to me as well. Be indulgent with my mistakes, and look to my intention of loving you and of serving you in the person of each one of your sick.

Lord, increase my faith, bless my efforts and my work, now and forever. Amen.

—Prayer from a home for children in Calcutta

8

"What We Do Is So Little!"

Who Can Criticize a Saint?

*A demagogue, an enemy of enlightenment,
a servant of worldly powers.*

— TV journalist Christopher Hitchens,
speaking of Mother Teresa

All things considered, isn't the attempt by the Missionaries of Charity a downright naive way to change the world? To be sure, the sisters work themselves to the bone; they give their energies to the limit. But is it all worth it? In a few chosen places the world is brighter — but what about the darkness elsewhere?

And, worse yet: aren't the amiable nuns doing a dangerous favor to those who are guilty of causing the miseries of society? Can't the internationally organized exploiters rest more easily, knowing that the unjust conditions won't be changing any time soon?

Again, aren't Teresa and her helpers making an enormous expenditure of labor and philanthropy just to cure symptoms, instead of pointing up the causes of poverty? Wouldn't it be more useful to brand, and fight against, lethal structures, murderous conditions of power, the unfair distribution of goods, instead of holding the hands of dying people?

There is just as much to criticize in Teresa's life as in the life of every other person who fought in an exposed position for an idea and whose statements were necessarily abbreviated and crude.

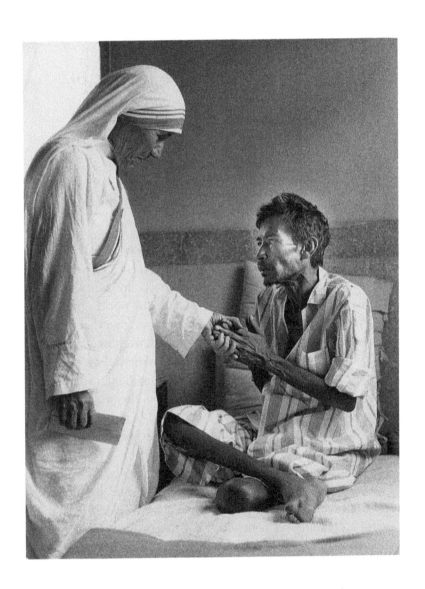

But that was because a message has to be pithy and terse to be rousing. One can get annoyed with her just as one can with all those who stood in the limelight when they worked, managed projects, and organized effective assistance. But they couldn't stop to engage in endless discussions of pros and cons because they necessarily had to act in a one-sided fashion.

One can shake one's head at the spiritual serenity with which, after the horrible explosion in the industrial city of Bhopal in 1984, Teresa advised the relatives of the killed, poisoned, and blinded workers "to forgive, forgive, forgive." She never uttered a word of accusation against the Dow Chemical Company, which had caused the catastrophe through sloppiness and profiteering.

One can, like the sharp-tongued American journalist Christopher Hitchens, lament the fact that on her countless trips Mother Teresa so often let herself be exploited by despots and dictators. She accepted honors from bloodstained tyrants like Jean-Claude "Baby Doc" Duvalier, instead of denouncing the violation of human rights by such figures.

In 1975 when Indira Gandhi declared a state of emergency in India and, according to Amnesty International, many of the at least fifteen thousand political prisoners in the country's detention centers were tortured and maimed, Teresa accepted from the hand of that same prime minister an honorary doctorate from the University of Visvabharathil. And even though she was on close personal terms with Indira Gandhi, she never spoke up in any way for the mistreated dissidents.

One can be of two minds about her image of women and her ideal of humility. One can argue that she had a dangerous theology, far too readily interpreting pain and suffering as a grace-filled gift of the Crucified Lord. Once she tried to encourage a cancer patient tormented by dreadful pain by telling her that Jesus must love her very much. "Your pains," she said, "are Jesus' kisses." Whereupon the moribund woman somewhat brusquely replied, "Then, Mother, beg Jesus to stop kissing me!"

One can ask critically whether Teresa didn't sometimes succumb to the temptation to misuse dying persons and undernourished children as "contemplative material for charity." One can blame her for dispensing with professional medical treatment of patients in her homes for dying, as the British physician Jack Preger did. (He had closely collaborated with Mother Teresa, but then broke with her and founded street clinics in Calcutta, where the very poor are supposed to get the same standard of medical care as the rich in hospitals.) One can ask whether the estimated $50 million in donations that Teresa's community gets every year shouldn't be concentrated on a few carefully chosen, optimally equipped projects, instead of letting the money dribble away on a thousand fleeting relief measures.

Healing People or Changing Structures?

All that may be right. But would those who know so precisely what roads to take to get out of poverty also be capable of taking hold of one of Teresa's stinking, worm-eaten patients and thereby changing the vexed relations between one human being and another? The only people who can believably cry out for justice are those who themselves lend a hand. The only ones who can seriously demand social change are those who have themselves begun to share. What's needed is not flaming appeals, but proof by example; and Mother Teresa showed what examples are supposed to look like.

Only those who share the wretchedness of the poor can set the wretched free. "How can I look the poor in the eye," Teresa asked, "how could I tell them, 'I love you and understand you,' if I didn't live as they do?"

The Australian businessman who saw the slums of Calcutta and gave Mother Teresa a very large check, only to say later that he was dissatisfied because he hadn't given anything of himself —

he had some notion of this. From then on he came to the home for the dying every day; he shaved the old men, who were already too weak to do it themselves, and spent time talking with them.

The usual sort of charity (Teresa liked to make this fine distinction) serves a purpose — to be sure, an admirable and necessary purpose — but love serves a person. A woman doctor who helped out in the home for the dying in Calcutta felt that it was an "incredible privilege" to be allowed to work there. She felt that this was the way to cross a gigantic gulf. "You know, then there no longer are those 'millions' of poor people; it's someone that you yourself have touched."

"What this is all about," Teresa said point-blank, "is the person. To be able to love the individual, we have to come into close contact with him or her. If we wait until we get the big numbers, we will lose ourselves in the numbers and never be able to show this love and respect for the person." She was convinced of it: Jesus would have died for just one person.

"Acknowledging the problem of poverty rationally," she pointed out, "doesn't mean that you understand it. Neither looking for the facts behind poverty in books, nor taking a trip through the slums, neither admiration nor pity, helps us to understand poverty or to recognize its good and bad sides. We have to plunge into it, live it, and share it with others."

Teresa has been chided for never touching upon social and economic structures, but limiting herself to appeals to personal lifestyle. Critics regret that her efforts at helping weren't co-ordinated in a comprehensive, politically oriented strategy of development to attack the causes of poverty. They point to honest alternative models such as the "social action groups," in which young Indian academics also live together with slum-dwellers, tenant farmers, and outcastes. Here at any rate there is an effort to build up effective self-help institutions or basic health services and to support hitherto powerless people in negotiations with the authorities and landowners.

Critics boldly demand that instead of just passing on donations and handing the hungry a fish, the Missionaries should teach people to use fishing rods so that in the future they can help themselves. Not bad, Mother Teresa used to reply. But, "The people who get picked up on the street or brought to our homes are too weak even to hold a fishing pole. If I give them a fish, I'm helping them to gain the strength that they can use tomorrow to go fishing."

Teresa never imagined that she could eradicate the slums of Calcutta — much less the slums of the entire world. So isn't what the Missionaries do just a drop in the ocean of the world's measureless misery? Absolutely — "But if we didn't release this one drop into the ocean of suffering," she said with disarming logic, "the ocean would be missing that one particular drop." Comparatively speaking, only a few individuals ever get into her elementary schools or homes for the dying. But if those buildings weren't there, then all those children would remain without education, and all those deathly ill people would die on the street. And if everyone poured a drop into the ocean, all the poverty in the world could be overcome.

"Social structures don't interest me," she bluntly admitted, and immediately accepted the fact that someone else might feel called by God to change those structures. But not Teresa — she didn't have "the time to think about grand programs." She saw it as her responsibility to help the individual person — and to concentrate on the flaws in that person, on egoism, greed, indifference. Putting it the old-fashioned way, on his or her quite personal *sin*.

Nonetheless, it was perfectly clear to her that the issue of structures was enormously important. "For us this individual needs a place to stay right now. I believe that our task is fulfilled in doing this. And, by doing our part, many people will be stimulated to take care of the other parts: to improve people's situation and to help them, to do away with poverty and hunger and nakedness."

In fact her example had repercussions. Upper-class Brahman women, for example, now sometimes go to the homes for the dying; they wash and feed those figures of wretchedness, on which they wouldn't have wasted a glance before.

Blocked Hearts Open Up

The Missionaries, Mother Teresa once said, should be "burning lamps," lighting the way for men and women. She herself was a shining light. An incarnate signal, showing that the desire to have things isn't the only possibility of human existence, nor does it truly make us happy. She was an unmistakable indication that human beings are brothers and sisters, and the outcasts are our siblings and friends.

When Malcolm Muggeridge was capturing the activities of the Missionaries on videotape, he found himself going through three phases: "The first was terror, mixed with pity; the second, pity pure and simple; and the third, which went far beyond pity, was something that I had never sensed before: the realization that these dying, down-and-out men and women, these lepers with stumps instead of hands, these unwanted children were not pitiable, repellent, or lost, but dear and precious; like old friends, brothers and sisters. How is one to explain this, the actual heart and mystery of the Christian faith? Caressing those beaten heads, touching those poor stumps, picking up in one's arms those children who had been dropped in garbage cans, because it was *his* head, just as it was *his* hands and *his* children, about whom he said that everyone who receives such a child in his name receives him."

What can today's completely ordinary people learn from this unique woman? Perhaps this: to deal mercifully with oneself and attentively, respectfully, and lovingly with others, especially with the weaker ones — who not infrequently reveal themselves to be

the really strong ones and richly benefit those who have decided
to cast their lot with them. Perhaps we can learn a whole new
equilibrium between giving and taking, and acquire the courage
to open up our anxiously blocked hearts. And we might remember heaven too, which often enough, busy as we are with all those
other things, we forget.

Dearest Jesus, help us,
to give out your fragrance,
wherever we go.
Flood our souls
with your spirit and life.
Penetrate our whole being
and take possession of it so completely
that our life is nothing
but a reflection of your shining
through us; and be in us in such a way
that every soul we meet
can sense your presence in our soul.
Let it look up and no longer see us,
but only you!
Abide with us, and we shall begin
to shine as you shine,
to shine so that we may be a light to others.
The light, Jesus, will come entirely from you,
nothing will be from us;
you will be the one
who shines on others through us.
So we wish to praise you in the way
that is dearest to you,
by shining on all men and women around us.
Let us preach you, not with words,

but by our example,
through the contagious power,
the sympathetic influence of our deeds,
the manifest fullness of love for you
that we bear in our hearts.
Amen.

Once she had passed eighty, Teresa was regularly given up for dead, this slight little nun who as a young teacher had had problems with her health and who later proved to be so tough. But she kept outwitting skeptical doctors and "concerned" journalists. She lived out her last years with a pacemaker in her heart; she had to be operated on during a trip to California. She was repeatedly taken to the hospital with pneumonia, malaria, blood clots in her brain, and chronic kidney disease. In 1996 within a period of ten days she suffered three heart attacks; she was given artificial respiration. After her heart had stopped, electroshock therapy brought her back to life.

The doctors had a hard time with her. When she was conscious, she refused expensive tests and specialists with the argument that she didn't want to have it better than the poor: "Let me die like those whom I have served!"

She had no fear of death. One curious person asked her whether she looked forward to the unknown afterlife. "Of course," Teresa answered with a gleam in her eye, "because then I'll be going home." Eternal life meant that "our soul goes to God, to be in God's presence, to see God, to speak with God, to go on loving him, with greater love."

When she was stricken with her final heart attack, all the doctors' skills could do nothing. On September 5, 1997, this restless woman's vital forces were exhausted. Teresa had reached the age of eighty-seven. Her adopted country gave her a state funeral.

How will the community do after her death? "If the order is God's work, then it will survive" — she was quite certain of that. Whether her personal accent would be preserved wasn't important. She had deliberately trained her sisters and brothers to work independently, to take their own responsibility. Even without *Mataji* they will handle the tasks of the community — if it is God's will.

"God will find another person," said Teresa as far back as 1989 at the age of seventy-nine, after suffering her first severe heart attacks, "much humbler, much more self-sacrificing, much more obedient; and the community will go on living." Someone like Teresa is irreplaceable. But anyone who has so indelibly marked a community as she did the Missionaries of Charity will never really go away.

"We had a young boy, whose parents were no longer living and whose grandmother was very old," says Sister Agnes, Teresa's very first and ever enthusiastic companion. His grandmother was worried about his future. She brought him to the sisters, and they took him in at Shishu Bavan. He graduated with good grades, went on to college, and later became a priest. When he was still a little boy, *Mataji* asked him on various occasions what he wanted to be when he grew up. He always looked at her with a combination of respect and romantic love, and he answered in a voice full of conviction: "I want to be Mother Teresa!" Saints never die.

Let us all together thank God for this wonderful opportunity to express our common joy that we are spreading peace, that we love one another and that we love peace, that the poorest of the poor are our brothers and sisters. . . .

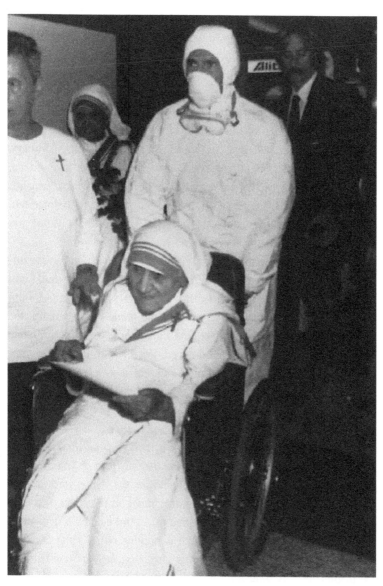

Arrival in the Rome airport, September 28, 1991, Mother Teresa stricken by illness.

How must we love? Love by giving; for God gave us his Son. He gave his life for us, and he continues to give; he gives here, everywhere, in our own life and in the lives of others. It was not enough for him to die for us. He wanted us to love one another; he wanted us to see him in others.

And to be sure that we understand what we need, he said that in the hour of death we would be judged by what we did for the poor, the hungry, the naked, and the homeless. He made himself hungry, naked, and homeless — hungry not just for bread, but for love; naked, not just without a piece of cloth, but without human dignity; homeless not just because he has no place to stay, but because he is forgotten, unloved, not cared for, lovable to no one. And he said: "What you have done to the least of my brothers, you have done to me."

Today, as I receive this great prize — I personally am quite unworthy of it — I am happy on account of our poor, happy that I can understand the poor, by which I mean the poverty of our people. I am thankful and very happy to receive it in the name of the hungry, the naked, the homeless, the cripples, the blind, the lepers. In the name of all those who feel unwanted, unloved, uncared for, those who have been ejected from society, who are a burden to society and excluded from everything. I accept the prize in their name, and I am sure that this prize will bring a new, understanding love between the rich and the poor. . . .

I will never forget how I once took a man in from the street. He was covered with maggots. His face was the only part of him that was clean. I brought the man in to the home for the dying, and he said only one sentence: "I have lived like an animal on the street, but now I will die like an angel, loved and cared for." And he died a wonderful death; he went home to God. Death is nothing but a going home to God. I sense that he rejoiced in this love, that he was wanted and loved, that he was someone for someone.

I have a conviction that I would like to share with you all: The greatest destroyer of peace today is the cry of the innocent, unborn child. When a mother can murder her own child in her own womb, what worse crime can there be, except for killing one another? It is even in Holy Scripture: "Even if a mother could forget her child, I will not forget." But today millions of unborn children are killed, and we say nothing. In the newspapers we read this and that, but no one speaks about the millions of little ones who were conceived with the same love as you and I, with the life of God. And we say nothing, we are mute.

For me the nations that have legalized abortion are the poorest of all. They are afraid of the little ones; they fear the unborn child. And the child must die, because they no longer wish to have this one child — not one child more — and the child must die. . . .

We fight abortion with adoption. With God's grace we will make it. God blesses our work. We have saved thousands of children; they have found a home where they are loved, where they are wanted, where they have brought joy.

And so I challenge you today, your Majesties, your Excellencies, ladies and gentlemen, all of you who have come from so many countries on earth: Pray that we may have the courage to protect unborn life. Here in Norway we now have the chance to speak out for it. . . .

I shall never forget a little child, a four-year-old Hindu boy. He had heard somewhere that "Mother Teresa has no sugar for her children." He went home to his parents and said; "I don't want to eat any sugar for three days." How much this little child loved. He loved until it hurt. Don't forget that there are many children, many women, many men in this world who don't have what you have, and remember to love these too, until it hurts.

Some time ago I picked up a child off the street; just looking at him, I could tell that he was hungry. I don't know how many days he had gone without having anything to eat. I gave him a peace of bread, and the little boy ate it crumb by crumb. I told the child: "Just eat the bread!" The child stared at me and said: "I'm afraid to eat the bread. I'm afraid that when it's gone, I'll be hungry again." . . .

The greatness of the poor is a reality. One day a gentleman came to me and said: "There's a Hindu family living in such and such a *place with eight children, and they have been going hungry for a long time." I took some rice and brought it there. While I was still there, the mother divided up the rice and went out with half of it. When she returned, I asked her what she had done. She answered: "They're hungry too." She knew that her neighbors, a Muslim family, were also going hungry. What most amazed me was not that she gave something to the neighbors, but that in her suffering, in her hunger she knew that somebody else was hungry. She had the courage to share and the love to share.*

That is what I wish from you: Love the poor and don't turn your back on them; for if you turn your back on the poor, then you are turning it on Christ. . . .

God bless you!

—From the address by Mother Teresa
at the awarding of the Nobel Prize for Peace, 1979

Pope John Paul II on Mother Teresa

*A Talk at the Angelus in Castel Gandolfo
on September 7, 1997*

Dear Brothers and Sisters!

At this moment of prayer, my heart bids me remember our dear sister, Mother Teresa of Calcutta, who just two days ago ended her long journey on earth.

I often had the opportunity of meeting her; and this slight figure, bent over in the service of the poorest of the poor, filled with an inexhaustible inner power — the power of the love of Christ — lives on in my memory.

She was a Missionary of Charity: her mission began every day, well before dawn, before the Eucharist. In silent meditation Mother Teresa of Calcutta heard within her the cry of Jesus on the cross: "I thirst." This cry, which she welcomed deeply in her heart, drove her out into the streets of Calcutta and all

the far-flung districts of the world to seek Jesus in the poor, the abandoned, and the dying.

Dear brothers and sisters, this nun, who all over the world is looked upon as a mother of the poor, gives everyone, believers and unbelievers, an eloquent example. She bequeaths to us a witness to the love of God, which she received and which transformed her life in complete dedication to her fellow men and women. She bequeaths to us a witness to the contemplation that becomes love and the love that becomes contemplation. Her deeds speak for themselves and testify to the people of our times the deep meaning of life, which unfortunately often seems to get lost.

She liked to repeat, "Serving the poor in order to serve life." Mother Teresa never missed a chance to bear witness in every way possible to love of life. She knew from experience that life itself, even amid trials and tribulations, takes on its full value when it experiences love. Following the Gospel, she made herself a "Good Samaritan" to every suffering, sick, and despised existence.

In the great heart of Mother Teresa there was a special place reserved for the family. "A family that prays," she said on the occasion of the first World Family Congress, "is a happy family." Even today the words of this unforgettable mother of the poor retain their unaltered power.

"In the family," she declared, "one loves as God loves: it is a love of sharing with one another. In the family one experiences the joy of loving and being loved. In the family one must learn to pray together. The fruit of prayer is faith, the fruit of faith is love, the fruit of love is service, and the fruit of service is peace."...

As we entrust to the Lord the greathearted soul of this humble, believing religious, we pray the holy Virgin Mary for help and consolation for her fellow sisters and for everyone in the whole world who has known and loved her.

Additional Reading

Christian Feldman
Saint John XXIII
An Unexpected prophet

Angelo Roncalli introduced himself to the crowds in St. Peter's Square on October 28, 1958 with the humble words, "I am called John." Already seventy-seven years old, he convened the Second Vatican Council in October of 1962, which would open wide the doors of the Church and change Catholic life forever, inside and outside the church. This biography, by reverend journalist, Christian Feldman, reveals the spiritual heart of this remarkable, thoroughly modern and thoroughly orthodox man.

978-0-8245-2042-7, pb

Robert Ellsberg
All Saints
Daily Reflections on Saints, Prophets, and Witnesses for our Time

"The lives of 365 saintly people…one for each day of the year—create a year's worth of reflections on the challenge of faith and holiness and true spiritual strength. The more recognized exemplars are included, of course – Augustine, Joan of Arc, and Teresa of Avila, along with such lesser knowns as Juan Diego and Elizabeth of Hungary. A year's worth of such inspiration is bound to make one a better person." — NAPRA *Review*

978-0-8245-1679-6, pb

Support your local bookstore or order
directly from the publisher at www.CrossroadPublishing.com
To request a catalog or inquire about
Quantity orders, e-mail
sales@crossroadpublishing.com

The Crossroad Publishing Company